SAFE SEX NEVER TASTED SO GOOD

™

A HEALTH COOKBOOK FOR THE 1990's

A Story Book Cookbook With Very Happy Endings

Written By: Susan Lee Mintz
as a "Word of Mouth" cookbook
May all your creams come true!

BONER APPETITE! ™

Boner Publications
Boca Raton, Florida

Safe Sex Never Tasted So Good.

Copyright (c) 1990
By Susan Lee Mintz

TM

1. Cookery I. Title
TX714.M557 1990

641.5 — dc20

90-188642
AACR 2 MARC

Library of Congress

Date of Registration June 29, 1990

Copyright Registration # TX 2 869 266

ISBN 0-9636037-0-1

Published by Boner Publications
P.O. Box 27-3883
Boca Raton, Florida 33427-3883
(407) 391-2058
Printed in the United States of America
First Printing May 1990
Fifth Printing December 1993
Jacket (cover) and illustrations by Mike Chapman

FORWARD

Welcome!

Enter into the world of "Safe Sex Never Tasted So Good"! I will take you on an eating and sexual experience, the likes of which you have never imagined! It is a journey of laughter, excitement, pleasure, and adventure. The foods are sensuous, tasty, and healthy, while the recipes are easy to prepare, incredibly edible, and pleasing to the palate.

This is the first of several books I plan to write. I will call them, "Boner Appetite Cookbooks"™. I want to become someone you can relate to and feel as close to as one of your family. I want to share my unusual sense of humor, my appreciation of good food, and all the fun that you can have by letting go..... in the kitchen!

This first book started out as a "joke" between several good friends. **It is no joke now!!** I am onto something that moves me as I have never been moved before, and I mean that, **LITERALLY!** All my years of discipline, nutrition, and exercise have finally come together in one incredible mental and physical package. <u>I want to give ME to YOU!</u>

Many publishers have had the opportunity to review my book, but feel they may have a hard time placing it in various "outlets" around the country. In doing my own research, I have found that although the publishers are hesitant to adopt my book, <u>the people want it!</u> Everyday I am receiving more and more requests for my book - from Florida to Washington; from New York to Los Angeles! I have decided to publish it myself. Through word of mouth and mail in orders, I decided to give the public the best collection of "Boner Appetite Cookbooks"™ they could ever want!

With your help, I'll market other Boner Appetite!™ products. I believe I'll have something that the public will heavily demand. I'll keep my costs down, because I want a lot of people to be able to buy this book for themselves, and ultimately, for a friend. It's a sharing book. If everyone buys one for that special occasion or for that special friend, I'll be able to show the "Big Boys" that the public is STILL smart enough to know a good thing!

BONER APPETITE!™ WILL BE HERE TO STAY!

Incidentally, when was the last time you took a cookbook to bed?

Susan Lee Mintz

CONTENTS: NAMES OF RECIPES

(Number in each category)

APPETIZERS: 21
SALADS, SALAD DRESSINGS, AND SAUCES: 22
ENTREES: 20
VEGETABLES, BEANS, RICE, PASTAS: 20
DESSERTS, BAKED GOODS, BREADS: 31

TOTAL RECIPES IN BOOK: 114

APPETIZERS:

SALADS, SALAD DRESSINGS & SAUCES:

ENTREES:

VEGETABLES, BEANS, RICE, PASTA:

DESSERTS, BAKED GOODS, BREADS:

PS: There is no index in the back of this book. Everything you get in this book is right up front...like me!

PLANNED DINNER SUGGESTIONS
(There are more with the Entrees)

IMAGINATION CAN CREATE MANY OTHER ORGANIZED MEALS SIMILAR TO THE FOLLOWING IDEAS. MAKE UP A MENU! SEND OUT INVITATIONS! HAVE A PARTY!

DINNER FOR A FIRST DATE:

EATIN' AT THE Y SPREAD/WITH ASSORTED CRACKERS, PITA BREAD, AND RICE CAKES
SHAKE IT BABY SALAD
FINGER LICKIN' LAMB CHOPS WITH BREATH MINT JELLY
SHAFT BITES
FUZZY NAVELS

DINNER THE 2ND TIME AROUND:

JIZZ WIZZ/ASSORTED CRACKERS
SEIZE ME SALAD
FONDLED BREAST OF CHICKEN
SCHMUCKS
MOON PIE OR MACAROON ME

LIGHT DINNER OF SALADS:

BLUE BALLS WITH ASSORTED CRACKERS AND VEGETABLES
TONGUED TUNA
STRADDLE ME SALAD
TITTY TOTS
GANG BANG MERINGUE PIE

MEXICAN FIESTA:

WHORETILLA CHIPS
PUMPIN' PICANTE
HOLEY GUACAMOLE
NASTY NACHOS
FORE-SKINNED CHICKEN
DOWN AND DIRTY RICE / OR POOPY PINTOS
WET DREAMS

ITALIAN FEAST:

CUNTALOUPE WITH ASSORTED MEATS
HOT-FLASHIN' ANTIPASTO
CHICKEN SCALLOPENIS
HAIR PASTA
SPERMONI

GETTING DOWN TO BASICS

TO GET FAMILIAR WITH THE VERSATILITY OF THIS BOOK AND THE INGENUITY OF MY RECIPES, I HAVE ORGANIZED 5 MEALS AS AN EXAMPLE OF THE DOZENS OF DINNERS THAT CAN BE PREPARED FROM MY BOOK. OTHER THAN THE DESSERTS, THIS IS A LOW-FAT, LOW-SALT, LOW-CHOLESTEROL, LOW-FAT PROTEIN, BIG CARBOHYDRATE COOKBOOK. IN MANY INSTANCES, THERE IS NO SUBSTITUTION FOR BUTTER, FLOUR AND SUGAR, BUT THESE ARE TO BE USED IN MODERATION.

UNLESS OTHERWISE STATED, THE FOLLOWING INGREDIENTS ARE STANDARD IN MY RECIPE PREPARATION:

Cream Cheese is Neufchatel

All Swiss and Cheddar Cheeses are reduced-calorie, lower-fat cheeses.

Yogurts are plain non-fat

Cottage cheese is 1% milk fat

Milk is skim milk

Sour cream is reduced-calorie (or use yogurt)

Oils include olive, peanut, safflower, canola and sesame

Tomato sauces or tomato products are no-salt

Brown sugar used is "25% less calorie light brown sugar"

Mayonnaise and salad dressing is reduced-calorie

All herbs and spices, vinegars, mustards, jalapenos, garlic, onions, fruits and vegetables should be used liberally.

I try to keep constant in my diet. My foods reflect the way I personally eat. Processed foods are much higher in fat and preservatives, and they are expensive. I tend to prepare my meals from scratch, thus keeping the quality and nutritional value at their highest level.

When I use any cooking oil in my home, and I have been doing so for 20 years, I only use the REAL thing... Peanut oil, sesame oil, safflower oil, olive oil, and butter. I do NOT try to cut my calories and substitute inferior products for the times I want quality. I have also NEVER traditionally fried anything. I lightly bread foods, saute' them in butter and olive oil (or other above oil), and drain. Try to use as little oil as possible.

Here's a Tip! I keep my olive oil in the refrigerator to prevent it from getting an odor. It gets cloudy and hard, but when brought to room temperature, it is fresh and natural. **I have found an interesting way to use less oil and still have quality and great flavor. Get a sprayer bottle and fill it with your favorite oil. Crush garlic cloves in it, and you now have an easy and economical way to spray a good oil on your salads or in your pans, to give it EXTRA zest!** I have several spray bottles labeled with my different oils and vinegars. It's practical, easy and convenient. I highly recommend the idea!

THE PERSONAL SIDE OF MRS. BONER

Welcome to Healthy Eating, with a "sexy" sense of humor! My background plays an important part in revealing why I feel about food the way I do, the preparation of it, and the health-side of it. It also helps to give insight to the type of person I am! Understanding all of this makes my recipes more appreciative, and my personal comments become more meaningful. This book contains healthy recipes, will teach about healthy eating, with a sense of humor, and will create a uniqueness that I know will be passed on to others.

I think there are two issues in life that most people take too seriously. The first one, of course is sex, and the second one is food. I personally don't understand the reasoning behind this dilemma. What is the worst thing that could possibly happen in either situation? You throw it out and start again! And, if you don't like it, don't do it! I've pulled several muscles in bed AND thrown a lot of food down my disposal. Sex has usually made me laugh, since my mind has always been quicker and more active than my body could respond. My performance has, shall we say, been given a possible 3 stars out of 5! My imagination exhausts me, the quickness of my wit and sharpness of my tongue sometimes astounds me, but the real kicker is - I could never write a sex manual on how to do it and keep them coming back!

I was born of Polish and Russian Orthodox Jewish descent. That in itself is a very heavy load to carry around! I lived with my paternal grandparents in the very early years of my life. I thought my grandmother was a whitefish because she was always grinding, scaling, and making gefilte fish! My father had a slaughterhouse in our garage behind our home on the Hudson River, in Troy, New York. Sundays were not spent like most normal children. I'd wake up early and watch in utter amazement, how much blood could come out of one small chicken, and what a putrid odor there was when the feathers were singed! But, it was fascinating, and I loved that time in my life. The chicken became a symbol to me and I knew I was bonded to them! My father was a kosher butcher and had a small meat market. He was so precise when he would carve an entire animal and prepare it for customers. I really grew up appreciating food preparation as an "art form". To this day, chicken is one of my favorite foods! The stage was set for me and all the characters were ready to start on an incredible journey. There was no turning back. I knew I'd be cooking up a storm the rest of my life!

I married when I was 22. My husband, Jeff, was 21 and never knew that I was a good cook. He never asked. He never assumed. I never really thought about it. It was just something that I felt I had to do. While I was a dental hygienist at the VA Hospital, he was teaching full time and going for a Master's Degree during the evening. I kept him well fed so he would work harder and get the hell out of school sooner! Naturally, I got all the freshest meat.... from my dad! I began sending away for cookbooks and pamphlets. I watched television shows on cooking. I began experimenting with different foods and recipes. On Sunday I would begin cooking in the morning and do dinners for the **entire** week! Jeff ate everything I put in front of him, no matter how "experimental" I became!! In fact, family, friends, and neighbors began hanging around our dinner table!

As our married life settled down, our sex life started to take a slight detour into "routine" and I began increasing my experimentation in the kitchen. Where I lacked in one area, I damn sure made up for it in the other. I was becoming a real gourmet chef - I felt I was worth my weight in gold... or in this case, in batter!

We moved from Albany, New York to Gainesville, Florida where Jeff went on for his Doctorate Degree. As a student's wife, I did not have much money, so again, I poured myself into experimental recipes. **Now** I was getting exposure to delicious "Redneck" North Florida cuisine..... swamp cabbage, hush puppies, okra, black-eyed peas, and catfish, to name a few. I was in heaven! More cookbooks! More pamphlets! More TV shows! And... I entered cooking classes. Jeff was the best fed student on campus, and when he graduated, I like to think it was my typing and cooking that got him through!

Our next move was to Houston, Texas. Here I learned the "Tex-Mex" cooking culture. It grabbed me so intensely and I found more flavors then I could ever imagine. Everyone was telling me to open my own restaurant, or write a cook-book. But still, the time wasn't right, and I just cooked for the fun of it. People were actually offering to pay me to cook for them! I could have begun a catering service!

Eating healthy had become part of our daily life. Neither of us had a weight problem. But as time went by, all of a sudden I found my body beginning to change, and I found myself looking like a turnip! It played havoc on me. I began to substitute different condiments and ingredients to compensate for calories, while still maintaining the great taste and nutrition. It was quite a challenge, because altering an ingredient could also alter the taste and consis-tency. More experiments began. But again, they paid off. My recipes were still delicious and now even <u>more</u> nutritious then ever!

Our next move was to Boca Raton, Florida, where I live today. The good life. Too good.... successful doctor's wife, money in my pocket, and time on my hands. Was I getting bored? Perhaps a little. I needed to fill a void. But, I wanted to do something beneficial - something useful. Then it happened...out of the blue! I decided what I needed to do... EXERCISE! I had found my niche! I began body building, weight-training, riding a stationary bike, etc. Discipline, individualism, restrictions in diet, and hard work could all be put together in one tight, well-balanced package. To make things even MORE exciting, **I had found <u>another</u> area of cooking with which I could experiment!** I realized that the <u>only</u> way to take fat off the body was to not take it in, and to work your "butt" off in a cardio program! In several months, my body (for the first time in 40 years) was taking shape. I was molding it into a super structure and was totally en-grossed in the process.

I started eliminating fat, salt, sugar, alcohol, fried foods, dairy products, and middle of the night snacks. I began reading labels more carefully and cooking in larger quantities, so I could snack on the "healthy" leftovers. All those years of experimenting, all the rearranging of recipes, and all the knowledge I acquired through the past 20 years had paid off. I found that simple food can be healthy, tasty, exciting, and easy to make. My mind and body had come together. I had come to a point in my life where the appreciation I had for life, my health, my body, the art of food preparation, and the excitement I felt had no limits. It was time to begin writing my own cookbook!

My friends and I gathered around the table one evening and listened to my ideas. With their help, we began "experimenting" with naming my recipes. We began brainstorming with sexy and dirty words and phrases which correlated with certain foods. The conversation became so comically "off-color", that we began a laughter that would have been contagious to anyone entering the room! "I've got it", I yelled. "I'll write a filthy, dirty, healthy, educational cookbook for anyone who wants to laugh all the way from the kitchen table to the bedroom!"

In my book, I decided to use personal notes for each recipe, as I changed the variety of it. I would share with the world the knowledge I had gathered all these years!

This book is full of recipes which have comical, sexy titles, but don't let the dirty words fool you or scare you off! The recipes are wonderfully delicious, and magnificently easy to prepare. They make up the wonderful, exciting contents of my cookbook which I call, "Safe Sex Never Tasted So Good."

Laugh! Be Healthy! Be Sexy!

Boner Appetite!™

DEDICATION

This book is dedicated to my husband, Jeff, who taught me the true meaning of the words "safe sex" - Don't Have Any!

And...

To our beloved dog, Spear, who for 14 years ate anything and everything I ever made!

To "Bunny" for her help and support!

To all my family and very few friends, "MY BONERS ARE YOUR BONERS"!

BONER APPETITE!™

A PERCENTAGE OF THE PROCEEDS FROM THE SALE OF "SAFE SEX NEVER TASTED SO GOOD" WILL BE USED TO PROVIDE FOOD FOR CHILDREN AND ADULTS WITH AIDS AND AIDS RELATED ILLNESSES. THANK-YOU FOR HELP-ING ME HELP THOSE IN NEED!   MRS. BONER

Appetizers
(Foreplay!)

EAT MY HOLE PIZZA

1 pita bread for 1 person

You can also make pizza on a bagel. The hole in the bagel gets filled with the ingredients and as it drips out you can stick your tongue in it and suck! You could probably get off on this way of making pizza, **if you concentrate!!** I like bagels, so I make my pizza this way a lot. Good as a "group game"!!

MARQUIS DE SADE'S MARINARA SAUCE - SEE RECIPE

Cheeses:

Cottage cheese, ricotta cheese, part-skim mozzarella, romano, low-fat Swiss or sapsago. Always shred cheeses and always look for part-skim and reduced-calorie or 1% milkfat products. Cut the fat wherever you can.

Toppings:

Ground cooked turkey, thinly slivered chicken or ham, sliced mushrooms, zucchini, tomatoes, onions, green peppers, sliced water-packed artichoke hearts, garlic, jalapeno peppers, tuna.

Note: Always thinly slice or - better yet - dice the fresh vegetables, since you will be baking this pizza only 10-15 minutes. You can pre-steam your vegetables or use leftovers. That way you are sure the "vegees" are done.

Seasonings:

Oregano, basil, thyme, rosemary, crushed red pepper flakes, garlic powder, onion powder, and popcorn seasonings that are salt free.

Preheat oven to 375 degrees

Cut pita bread into 2 flat breads, carefully cutting around edges. Spread with tomato sauce. Top with cheeses of your choice. Finish off with your favorite toppings. Bake on a non-stick baking sheet at 375 degrees for 10-15 minutes or until bubbly. (Be sure that the edges don't burn). Add a little extra romano when finished.

SUGGESTION: Use various pita breads on the market, i.e. whole wheat, onion, sesame, garlic, regular.

Note: Pita bread comes in small sizes called "Pitettes." They are cute, but a "pain in the ass" to cut!!

BEAT MY MEATBALLS

1 pound of ground turkey or any good ground beef makes 12-16 meatballs

(I like my balls big! So what else is new?!) But, ball size is your preference. It's what's in them that counts. Or, it's what they're on that matters!!

2 pounds of ground turkey
1/2 cup fresh bread crumbs. I use slices of day old 40 calorie light bread.
1/4 cup chopped onion
2-3 cloves garlic, minced
Black pepper to taste

Optional: I add chopped spinach to my meatballs. I think it gives them great flavor and texture. You can use this recipe for your turkey burgers or a meatloaf.

Mix all ingredients together in a large bowl. Using wet hands, make balls according to the size you want. In a large Dutch oven or frying pan, brown meatballs on all sides several minutes until cooked through. Drain and use for your favorite recipe. If using in a sauce, add them to the sauce and cook longer to blend flavors. Do this for spaghetti and meatballs.

Add the balls to your tomato sauce and serve on hoagie rolls, pita, or anything you want.

These balls will be as easy to eat as your date! My husband loves them. After I cook them in the sauce, I put them in a casserole dish. He munches on them like popcorn! We raid the refrigerator and pop a few like cookies! If you do not want the spinach, just use onion, garlic, and good bread crumbs.

SUGGESTION: As an appetizer, make smaller balls. Serve with sweet and sour sauce, tomato sauce, salsa, or blue cheese dressing.

Note: See what a basic recipe can do: Main meal, sandwich, appetizer, snack. This recipe is basic and versatile, just like your author! See how clever you've become!! Mrs. Boner does NOT want you to get fancy with this recipe. If you are going to use a good sauce and pasta, she wants you to just taste the flavor of how good turkey can be when it's moist and prepared with garlic and onions.

NASTY NACHOS

Serves 6-8 as an appetizer. Serves 2 after great sex; serves 1 when miserable and alone. **I eat batches of these alone!!**

Whoretilla chips. See index for home-made tortilla chip recipe/or use 1 large bag of good tortilla chips. Get them from a Mexican restaurant.

1 can refried beans. If you have leftover beans, put them in a blender with some onion and garlic powders, and a little hot sauce. Seasoned mashed-up beans are great!

4 ounces shredded Monterey jack cheese or sharp Cheddar or use a combination of both.

1 can chopped green chilies or jalapeno slices
Taco sauce or a jar of salsa (see index for Pumpin' Picante Sauce)
Imitation or lite sour cream or plain yogurt

Note: You can use tomatoes and green chilies that come mixed together in a can.

Preheat broiler

Line a large pie plate or baking dish with tortilla chips. I like to overlap them because it looks more like a pie shell and everything can get gooey and run on each other. Spoon refried beans over chips. Layer next with chopped green chilies and top with salsa. Sprinkle with shredded cheese. Broil about 3 inches from heat for several minutes till heated through and cheese is melted.

Serve with sour cream, yogurt, extra jalapeno slices, Holey Guacamole (see index for recipe).

EXTRA TOPPINGS: CHICKEN STRIPS, GROUND BEEF, SHRIMP, OLIVES

Basic layering: chips, beans, chilies, salsa, cheese. Add sour cream and guacamole when serving. If using any other toppings, make sure all meat is browned and fat removed, that the shrimp is cooked, and chicken strips should be warmed previously. Broiling really gets everything soft and you can just pull the chips apart. I always use extra nacho slices on mine but I like very spicy, highly seasoned foods. It is a fun, quick dish to put together for friends.

Note: If you are making Mexican appetizers, I think that it is so easy to make your own Guacamole, Picante Sauce, Refried Beans, Whoretilla Chips, and Nachos. All recipes are in this book. Poopy Pintos can be drained and mashed. They would make a great dip. Fried Tattas can also be spread on chips. You have a Mexican buffet in this sexy, healthy book!

HOLEY GUACAMOLE

Yields 2 cups

Avocados are delicious and nutritious. This recipe is so tasty and really cuts down on the amount of avocado used, so you can have your holey and eat it too! However, do remember that unless you are going to put avocados on your face as a skin mask, they are lethal in fat content! **Stay away from these beauties if you want thighs that do not move, when you are lying down and playing dead!**

1 large ripe avocado - mash it with a fork
1 cup (1% milkfat) cottage cheese
2 cloves garlic, minced
1/2 cup non-fat plain yogurt or lite sour cream
1/4 cup chopped green olives. Drain and wash them in cold water.
1/3 cup chili sauce

Put everything in the food processor. Whip until creamy and blended. Chill several hours before serving.

SUGGESTION: Great as a dip on vegetables, baked potatoes, on your Nasty Nachos, or in tomato cups. Also use as a filler for deviled eggs, a topping on your turkey burgers, or as a salad dressing.

Note: Again, see where one recipe can serve a multitude of sins!
This is how I cook. Make a batch of something up and then rearrange it to suit your needs.

SUGGESTION: Throw a can of tuna in this recipe and a little minced onion and you have another concoction that is great as a dip! Avocado tuna dip! Try it on your baked potato with extra garlic and a little shredded Swiss. Come in your pants and don't stop!

Note: To the lucky and very smart people who have purchased this book (and others to follow!), you are beginning to rock and roll. You are now becoming brilliant and very creative. I am proud of you.

Special Note to Girls:

Girls! You are beginning to enter a new world. You will be ready to change your hair color and hike up those skirts.

Special Note to Men:

Men! Keep your zippers up. Food is where the real women are.

PUMPIN' PICANTE

Yields 2 cups

Humpin' or pumpin', this "hot dish" is definitely going to be fire down below!! Great on anything! And I mean... <u>ANYTHING!!</u>

2-3 large tomatoes, coarsely chopped
1 tablespoon olive oil
1/2 cup chopped sweet onion
2 tablespoons fresh parsley or coriander, chopped
1 jalapeno-washed, seeded and diced; or 1 small can chopped green chilies
2-3 cloves garlic, minced
1/2 cup finely chopped green pepper, optional
1 tablespoon lemon juice, fresh
1/4 teaspoon sugar
1/2 teaspoon black pepper
1/2 teaspoon cumin - <u>IMPORTANT</u>.

Mix altogether.

This may seem like a lot of ingredients, but the freshness of this salsa is great. Keep it chunky. If you are making it in the food processor, don't liquefy it. It tastes and looks better chunky.

Serve with Whoretilla Chips and Holey Guacamole. See index.

LIP DRIP DIP

Yields 3 Cups

I wanted this dip to taste like fish, so I used salmon. Substitute tuna, herring fillets (well drained), or any of the seafood blends that are on the market. It is a dip for crackers, vegetables, or on baked potatoes or bagels.

1 (15-1/2 oz.) can salmon, boned, flaked, and thoroughly drained
1/4 cup finely chopped celery
1/4 cup finely chopped red onion
2 cloves garlic, minced
1 tablespoon fresh parsley
1 tablespoon fresh lemon juice
1 teaspoon paprika
1/4 teaspoon Worcestershire sauce (optional)
1 cup (1% milkfat) cottage cheese
2 tablespoons reduced-calorie mayonnaise
2 tablespoons chili sauce

Put all ingredients in the food processor and whip until blended. When creamy, place in a serving bowl and garnish with extra parsley. Chill several hours before serving.

SUBSTITUTIONS: Two 6-1/2 oz. cans of water-packed tuna, drained and flaked; 2 cups chopped seafood blend; 2 cups chopped shrimp; 2 cups jarred herring fillets (fillets that are in a jar, not fillets that have been tossed around!).

Note: Just make sure to drain the fish thoroughly before you process it. This dip should not be watery. If you want to use 4 ounces of Neufchatel cream cheese to make this recipe more of a spread, it's great on bagels. In fact, with the salmon, onion and other ingredients, you have a lox spread made up for a morning brunch. A very easy and tasty dip which is low-calorie and seasoned up or down to YOUR preference.

FINGER FOODS

**Serve both of these foods together. Deviled Eggs AND Potato Appetizers. Pretty!
And, real easy to prepare. <u>Great finger foods!</u>** Two easy hand-to-mouth appetizers.
What comes after the hand is up to you! A great way to start a romantic dinner!

HOOTERS

DEVILED EGGS

Serves 8 Appetizer Portions

8 hard-boiled eggs. Allow to cool.
1 can sardines, drained thoroughly
1/4 cup (1% milkfat) cottage cheese
Garlic powder, onion powder, pepper to taste
1 teaspoon lemon juice
1/2 teaspoon Worcestershire sauce

Peel eggs. Cut in half. <u>THROW AWAY THE YOLKS OR GIVE THEM TO THE CAT!</u>
Combine all the other ingredients in food processor until very creamy. Place on egg half.
Adjust all ingredients to suit your taste. Sprinkle with paprika.

KNOCKERS

CAVIAR NEW POTATO SLICES

Serves 8 Appetizer Portions

8 medium new potatoes - leave skin on them
Red or Black Caviar
1/4 cup chopped onion
1/4 cup low-calorie or lite sour cream, or non-fat plain yogurt

Boil new potatoes for about 25 minutes in water. Drain and allow to cool. Cut off ends
and cut into 1/2 inch slices. Top with yogurt, sour cream, chopped onion, and a
teaspoon of caviar.

Garnish with scallions and cherry tomatoes.

*Note: Place both the sardine stuffed eggs and caviar potatoes on the same serving dish.
It's an eye opener!*

BURNING BUTTOCKS

24 Buttocks

This recipe is dedicated to a woman who is dead. She had heat rash between her thighs and was always saying that her buttocks were burning! **The name will remain anonymous to protect her family.** Hope all your buttocks burn after this fiery Mexican appetizer chicken dish!

24 chicken drumsticks

Leave the fat on or you will be pulling skin all day. If you have to "watch" the fat, don't make this recipe. I really like it for a large crowd. It is very elegant.

2 cups crushed low-salt corn chips or taco chips
1 jar medium or hot taco or picante sauce
2 tablespoons chili powder
1 tablespoon garlic powder
Garnish: jalapenos and parsley sprigs

Note: Holey Guacamole or Pumpin' Picante (see index), can be used as a side dipping sauce if you like.

Preheat oven to 350 degrees

Spray baking pans or cookie sheets with non-stick cooking spray. In a large bowl, place crushed corn chips, chili powder, and garlic powder. In another bowl, moisten chicken in taco or picante sauce. Remove chicken from sauce and roll in corn chip mixture until well-coated. Bake 30-45 minutes or until brown and done.

Serve with garnishes and....OLE'!! (O! L-a-y)

SUGGESTION: You can do this same dish with pretzels (no salt ones). It's DELICIOUS! You can also use chow mein noodles and salt-free potato chips. Check the fat content. Keep it low. Use tomato sauce or sweet and sour sauce instead of picante. Chicken drums are a beautiful appetizer, and easy to eat with your hands which leaves your feet free! But for the real burning of your buttocks, I suggest you keep the Mexican recipe for this chicken.

HOT LIPS/HOT HIPS

Makes 40 Appetizers

Mexican food is my favorite. I think the jalapeno pepper is one of nature's most valuable treasures. Garlic is second, and chicken is third. For anyone who can't stand the fire down below, I would suggest that you do NOT make this recipe. Stuffed jalapenos are very popular. They are versatile, inexpensive and available. Sounds like your author! <u>I will give you several versions that are very low-calorie and will bring a grown man to his knees and a woman begging for mercy!!</u>

20 fresh jalapeno peppers cut in half, seeded, and steamed for 2 minutes in boiling water. This is not necessary, but some people like them softer. Sometimes I boil them and sometimes I don't.

4 ounces Neufchatel cream cheese
1/3 cup chopped green onion
1 teaspoon garlic powder -or- 1 tablespoon fresh chopped garlic
    (I'm real serious when I do this version!)
1 tablespoon chopped cilantro or parsley
2 ounces reduced-fat Cheddar cheese, grated

Combine all ingredients in a bowl and mix well. After jalapenos have cooled, stuff with mixture. Wrap in plastic wrap and chill several hours. That's it!!

<u>Other Mixtures:</u>

4 ounces Neufchatel cream cheese
1/2 cup crushed pineapple, well drained
2 tablespoons chopped red pepper
1 tablespoon chopped cilantro or parsley

4 ounces Neufchatel cream cheese
1 can baby shrimp
1 tablespoon lemon juice
1 tablespoon garlic powder
1 tablespoon chopped cilantro or parsley

4 ounces Neufchatel cream cheese
1/2 cup chopped cooked chicken
1 tablespoon fresh chopped garlic
1 tablespoon chopped parsley or cilantro
1/4 cup chopped fresh tomato
1 tablespoon blue cheese, crumbled

SUGGESTION: Use all the above stuffings on baked potatoes, bagels, rice cakes, or as a spread on celery, cucumber slices or on any vegetable you like. Also, you have 4 cream cheese spreads here that can be rolled into small balls. Or, make a cheese log and serve with crackers or party rye!

BUTT HOLES

Serves 6 (24 stuffed mushrooms)

How many of you would call **YOUR** stuffed mushrooms "butt holes??" Button mushrooms will <u>head</u> start ANY Italian banquet!

24 medium to large mushroom caps. Buy whole mushrooms with stems and
    chop stems to use with filling.
3/4 cup fresh Italian bread crumbs or any day old (40 calorie) bread made into crumbs
1 stalk celery, finely chopped
1 large onion, chopped
3 cloves garlic, minced
1/4 cup fresh chopped parsley
Chopped mushroom stems
1 tablespoon black pepper
1 tablespoon mixed Italian herbs, or 1 teaspoon each thyme, basil, oregano
1/4 cup tomato paste
2 tablespoons olive oil and 2 tablespoons butter or margarine

Optional: Low-calorie Italian dressing

Note: Some of the seasonings can be changed to suit your taste and you may have more stuffing left over. I sprinkle the caps with low-calorie Italian dressing and garlic powder. Makes caps very flavorful.

Preheat oven to 350 degrees

Thoroughly wash mushrooms, remove stems from caps, and wrap caps in paper towels to dry. In a large frying pan, combine butter and olive oil. Saute' the celery, onion, garlic, parsley, herbs, and mushroom stems. Cook 8-10 minutes, stirring occasionally to prevent sticking. Add a little water, if necessary. (I like the stuffing drier). When cooked, turn off heat and add bread crumbs. Mix thoroughly. Then stir in tomato paste.

Spray baking pan with non-stick cooking spray. Stuff caps with mixture. Bake for 12-15 minutes. Remove and garnish with additional parsley, lemon wedges, or sprinkle with parmesan cheese.

They do taste better when cooled. My friends have eaten these too hot - too soon, and burnt their mouths! But, to most of my friends, I'm glad it happened! Remember - they DO taste better when cooled!

<u>Suggested Meal:</u>   Butt Holes
Hot-Flashin' Antipasto
Chicken Scallopenis
Spermoni

NIPPLE NUGGETS

4-6 Appetizer servings

Having lifted weights for a few years, these are about the size of my breasts! Not big, just meaty!! Small enough, though, for one **good** bite!

2 (1 lb.) cans of beets - whole and drained
1 large sweet onion, cut into thin rings
2 cloves garlic, minced
4 tablespoons Balsamic vinegar or any good garlic or wine flavored vinegar
1 teaspoon black pepper
1/2 cup olive oil
1 teaspoon dry mustard

Place drained beets in a large bowl. Toss with all the other ingredients. Chill several hours or overnight. Drain. Serve with apple wedges, whole wheat crackers, large unsalted beer pretzels and deviled eggs.

Note: Stick with curly cocktail picks. What an appealing appetizer! And... very low-calorie when the oil is drained off.

If using fresh beets, cook 30-40 minutes until tender. Slice or cut into wedges. Beets are not used very much for appetizers, but they should be.

TM

JIZZ WIZZ

Yields 2 cups

<u>Imagination!</u> This is the key word for this spread. I do not know why I named this mushroom spread this, but who cares?

1 pound fresh mushrooms, chopped fine. Blot between paper towels.
2 tablespoons butter or olive oil
1/2 cup chopped onion
2 cloves garlic, minced
1 tablespoon fresh parsley, chopped
1 teaspoon black pepper
1 tablespoon lemon juice
1 tablespoon liquid hot pepper seasoning

In a large frying pan, saute' mushrooms, onion, garlic and seasonings in olive oil. Cook for several minutes, stirring occasionally. Transfer to a serving dish. Serve with rice cakes, pita bread, melba toast or crackers.

Note: Hot Mushroom Spread is <u>Delicious</u> on Baked Potatoes!!

SUGGESTION: If you let it chill, you can incorporate 4 ounces of Neufchatel cream cheese and make it a super spread. Use on top of celery, or with apple wedges or crackers. Maybe we should call this recipe "Gee-Wizz"!

EATIN' AT THE Y SPREAD

Yields 1 Cup, (plus some)

You like this title? <u>Me too!</u> Had lots of "head trips" trying to find something that would fit into this slot! But, it did happen. It's good and very tempting! Pimento-cheese spread just for you. The pepperocini and pimento make this basic dip great. **No better eating at any Y in town!**

1 cup (1% milkfat) cottage cheese
1 pepperocini - cut in half, seeded, and chopped
1 (2 oz.) jar chopped pimento
1 clove garlic, minced
1 tablespoon chopped scallion
1/2 teaspoon liquid from pepperocini

Place all ingredients in food processor and whip for 5-10 seconds.

SUGGESTION: Serve with assorted vegetables, rice cakes, pita pockets, small bagels, or on baked potatoes. Or, you can toss it in your favorite pasta. Sounds bazaar? <u>It is delicious on fetticini noodles too... hot or cold!</u>

SMEGMA SURPRISE

Makes 8-12 large turnovers. Serves 4-6 people as a hot appetizer.

This recipe goes back 20 years. I was a blushing bride and made these for a dinner party. I smile then... I'm smiling now. It's a turnover, and, inside you have a stuffing of feta cheese and spinach. That's the cheesy surprise!

2 cans crescent dinner rolls
1 package of chopped spinach, drained between paper towels to get all liquid out.
1 container of ricotta cheese or part-skim feta cheese.
    (Cottage cheese can also be used).
1 egg
1/4 cup skim milk. If you want a drier mixture, use less milk.
Dash nutmeg, dill, garlic and onion powder

Preheat oven to 375 degrees

Combine drained spinach, cheese, egg, enough milk to moisten, and spices. Mix thoroughly. If mixture looks too wet, place a paper towel over it and pat dry. Take 2 crescent rolls and press along perforations to make a square. Place 2 tablespoons of mixture in center of one triangle. Fold 1/2 of the dough over the other half to make a turnover. Press edges all around to seal. Bake on a non-stick baking sheet for 20-25 minutes at 375 degrees until golden brown. Let cool for 5 minutes before removing and serving.

SUGGESTION: Use this basic filling in "twice-baked" potatoes, stuffed in large mushroom caps (broil them), inside a rolled chicken breast, and finally, you can mix with noodles for a unique noodle pudding.

BANGERS

24 Servings

What cookbook would be complete without a good bang? If there is a low-calorie and versatile appetizer, it is a "banger"! These shish-ka-bob treats are so good that the gang will get a bang out of them!!

8 medium to large shrimp
8 boneless chicken chunks or strips
8 large chunks of a turkey coldcut or turkey breast

Any combination of a low-calorie, low-fat meat or seafood will do

24 skewers - can be purchased in any gourmet store or some supermarkets. Wood ones about 8 inches long are perfect. **Why settle for six inches if you can get ate (eight)!**

Pineapple chunks
Green or red pepper chunks
Large mushroom caps
Cherry tomatoes

Use plum preserves, pineapple preserves, peach preserves or any sweet and sour sauce or dressing. Make your own with a little extra ginger or soy sauce, mustard, pineapple syrup, garlic powder, etc. Make your marinade and broil.

Preheat broiler for 10 minutes so it is very hot.

When marinating any dish, it is always better to marinate several hours in the refrigerator, and let warm up to room temperature before broiling. Turn once in a while so the marinade blends with the food.

Arrange any combination of the above on skewers. Broil 5 minutes. Turn, baste, and broil 5 minutes more or until browned and done. Oven temperatures vary depending on how close to the heat your rack goes. Just watch it. About 10 minutes is average. Reserve extra marinade and brush on before serving.

Garnish with lemon slices, parsley, or extra cherry tomatoes.

Note: Shish-ka-Bobs are a wonderful appetizer, easy to eat, and no mess afterwards for the cook!

THE SIX INCHER

Serves 6

1 SIX INCHER FOR 2 PEOPLE

3 cucumbers (about six inches long)

Not to be confused with the "Grinder". This is the six incher, a more delicate warm up, appetizer, and pre-grinder dish. <u>You got to get loose before the main event!</u> Stretch your muscles before you run!

3 large cucumbers, pared, cut in half lengthwise, and seeded.
    Blot with paper towels to remove moisture.
4 ounces Neufchatel cream cheese, or
    1 cup (1% milkfat) cottage cheese, or a combination of both.
1 can baby shrimp, or 1 can tuna, or 1 cup seafood blend, or cooked chicken, ham, etc.
2 tablespoons chopped scallion
1 tablespoon chopped fresh parsley
1 teaspoon pepper
1 teaspoon garlic powder

Mix all ingredients together, except cucumbers.

Spread mixture in cucumber halves. Wrap in plastic wrap and chill for several hours. Cut into smaller 2 inchers! You can use any combination of cheeses, seasonings, and fillers, but inside a cucumber you save a lot of calories and it looks very pretty if you are making it with an appetizer tray.

Note: You can stuff celery, mushroom caps, or cherry tomatoes with this mixture. Because you change the vegetables and the fillings, <u>it looks like you have been fussing for hours!</u>

SCROTUM SNACKS

24 Snacks

This recipe is dedicated to my sister Irma, who loves **SNACKS,** and to everyone else who loves scrotums! For all you wonderful and unique people, this one's for you!!

Begin with: 24 chicken wings

Don't disjoint and don't remove fat. We are going all out and I want you to taste some fat in this appetizer recipe. You have been so disciplined and stuck to my suggestions for a great body and you used your dirty mind, that I now want you to enjoy these scrotum baby's **all the way!!**

Ingredients: adjust to suit your taste

1/2 cup ketchup or hot barbecue sauce
1 tablespoon red wine or garlic flavored vinegar
2 tablespoons light brown sugar, 25% reduced-calorie variety
2 tablespoons stone ground mustard
1 tablespoon chili powder
1 tablespoon Worcestershire sauce
2 garlic cloves, finely minced
2 green onions, finely chopped

Preheat oven to 375 degrees

Take a large cookie sheet or baking pan and spray with non-stick cooking spray or line with foil. Several hours before serving, mix all ingredients in a very large bowl and add chicken wings. Keep tossing to really blend flavors.

Place chicken wings on pan and bake for 20 minutes. Turn and bake 20 minutes more. If wings get too browned, cover with foil. Baste once. When transferring to platter, top with a little extra sauce. Garnish with parsley or jalapenos for those who like a spicy flavor.

SUGGESTION: You can use this basic barbecue recipe for any dish...chicken, ham slices, and ribs. I cut spareribs into small bite size pieces and serve them with pineapple slices on top. Chicken wings are nice served in a chafing dish so they can stay hot. Lamb riblets are not popular with many people, but if you know your guests like lamb, then it also makes for a nice change.

BLUE BALLS

Yields 3 cups

You choose the size of the balls: small, medium or large.

This is a very interesting recipe. It uses lower-fat cheeses and grated fresh vegetables. It is very pretty and different.

1 (8 oz.) package softened Neufchatel cream cheese
4 ounces reduced-fat sharp Cheddar cheese, shredded
4 ounces blue cheese, crumbled
1/2 cup grated carrot
1/2 cup grated zucchini
1/2 cup chopped green pepper
1 tablespoon chopped onion
1 tablespoon chopped garlic
1 tablespoon chopped fresh parsley

Garnish: chopped pecans, walnuts, or raisins

The important part is to squeeze all the moisture out of the vegetables. In a large bowl, combine all the ingredients except garnish and then... **play ball!**

SUGGESTION: To take this recipe one step further, serve on melba toast, pita wedges, or whole wheat crackers. Or, take a small ball and stuff it into a mushroom cap and serve with a frilly toothpick. Or, top each small ball with a cherry tomato and turkey chunk. Or, spread it inside celery stalks. Or, stuff in cucumber boats.

You can use any combination of vegetables you want, but the secret is to keep the fat content down in this recipe. Everyone is on the band wagon to stop eating cheese, and to some extent this is good. But, so many of the cheeses today are reduced-fat, and considering you don't sit down and devour the entire recipe, how bad is a small ball or two?

Note: This recipe used as a spread is wonderful on a toasted bagel for lunch or on top of a baked potato!

CUNTALOUPE WITH ASSORTED MEATS

Serves 8

Every good melon needs some meat wrapped around it once in awhile!! This favorite appetizer is juicy and hardly unappealing, if you know what I mean. Choose your melon and use meats that are mostly turkey coldcuts. Ham and other coldcuts have a high sodium content, but I think that this appetizer can also be used with assorted breads and low-fat cheeses for a nice lunch.

1 large melon cut into 8 wedges
Assorted coldcuts or preferably turkey breast
Lime wedges, parsley, cherry tomatoes, and pretty toothpicks

Cut melon. Wrap meat around wedges, secure with toothpicks and add garnishes.

Cuntaloupe, horneydew, persion, casaba... You like it? You buy it!

69 SPREAD

Yields 2 cups

69 was the year I got married, so I really was spreading them then!! Enough fish jokes, so let's get into something full bodied and substantial! You will hear this recipe called many things, from hummus or chick-pea dip, to garbanzo bean spread. Right - on all of the above! Every Mediterranean culture has their own bean collection, and this is mine. It is delicious, full of carbohydrates, and can be used as a main spread for pita or bagel sandwiches, or open-faced on cucumber and tomato slices. A little raw onion is nice too.

1 small onion, chopped
2 cloves garlic, minced
3 tablespoons olive oil
2 cups garbanzos - canned ones are fine. Save liquid. Mash with fork.
2 tablespoons chopped fresh parsley
Juice of one lemon
1/2 teaspoon of each of the following: pepper, cumin, basil, oregano.

Saute' onion and garlic in olive oil until golden brown. In your food processor, whip this mixture with all the other ingredients. Blend until the consistency is like mashed potatoes. Add a little of the garbanzo liquid if mixture is too thick.

Note: You may add 1/4 cup toasted sesame seeds to this mixture for a different flavor. To toast sesame seeds, sprinkle on baking sheet and bake for 10 minutes at 350 degrees.

Salads, Dressings, and Sauces
(Catch Your Breath!)

THE MARQUIS DE SADE'S MARINARA SAUCE

He would have beat himself black and blue for this recipe!
I would never have given that pervert such a full bodied sauce!!

Yield: A Lot! Enough for any recipe and then some!

1/3 cup olive oil
1 large onion, chopped very finely
1/2 pound sliced mushrooms, optional if you do not like mushrooms
1 pound ground turkey or good ground sirloin, optional if you do not like meat
4-6 cloves garlic, minced
1 large can Italian plum tomatoes. Use liquid in sauce.
1 (12 oz.) can tomato paste
2 tablespoons chopped fresh parsley
1 tablespoon sugar
1 tablespoon salt
1 tablespoon mixed Italian herbs (oregano, basil, thyme). I add more of these to sauce.
1/2 teaspoon black pepper
1/2 teaspoon crushed red pepper flakes (optional)
1 bay leaf
1/4 cup burgundy wine, (optional)

In a large frying pan, in hot olive oil, saute' onion, garlic, mushrooms, and turkey. Cook until vegetables are golden brown and meat has been thoroughly cooked. Drain excess fat and oil from mixture. Transfer to Dutch oven or large pot. Mix all the other ingredients. Mash tomatoes if they are in large pieces. Add 12 oz. of water to sauce. I like thick sauce, so I am careful about adding extra liquid.

Heat until boiling. Cover, reduce heat and simmer, stirring occasionally - about one hour. Taste and adjust seasonings. Remove bay leaf. Cool.

It freezes great and is very tasty. This is Mrs. Boner's favorite tomato sauce and I use it for almost all my recipes. But, as long as the fat and sodium contents are not excessive in any tomato sauce, use the one you like the best.

Note: **Remember, red sauces are better for you than white sauces.** White sauces usually have butter and flour. Red sauces have olive oil, tomatoes, garlic and spices. Even when you eat out, ask for red sauces.

SUGGESTION: Add more garlic and red pepper. We like spice, so I will always add more seasonings than most people. But that adds more flavor, thereby cutting back on the fat and heavier ingredients. That's my secret... Spices, herbs and wine, garlic, onion, pepper.... low-calorie **AND** flavorful!

Boner Appetite!™ It's going to get even better! They are on their knees just begging for more!

DON'T RUSH ME DRESSING

Yields 1 to 1-1/2 cups

This dressing means what it says. It takes a little longer to "make", but I'm worth waiting for!

1/2 cup (1% milkfat) cottage cheese
1/2 cup non-fat plain yogurt
1/4 cup chili sauce or sweet pickle relish
1/4 cup tomato sauce, plain variety
1 tablespoon chopped scallion
1 tablespoon chopped green pepper
1 tablespoon chopped red pepper
1 clove garlic, minced
1 hard-boiled egg (white only), chopped
1/2 tablespoon black pepper
1/2 teaspoon paprika

Put all ingredients in blender or food processor. Whip the shit out of it! Refrigerate and ....enjoy! Don't rush me about anything... **ANYWHERE!! ANYTIME!!**

Note: If you need a little salt in this one, add some chopped celery or 1 tablespoon red caviar. Serve extra caviar on side. Red only.

FINGER SAUCE

Yields 1 cup

Finger sauce should be white. I wanted a "Louis sauce" in here for crab and sea-food, but I didn't think that a Louis could be white, so this is MY version of tartar sauce for seafood.

1/2 cup (1% milkfat) cottage cheese
1/2 cup non-fat plain yogurt
1 tablespoon chopped scallion
1 small dill pickle, chopped
1 tablespoon chopped fresh parsley
1 teaspoon black pepper
1 teaspoon lemon juice
1 tablespoon chopped capers.
     (This is the best... little chopped green things in here...so flavorful!)

Whip it all up, chill, and serve on seafood, vegetables, poached chicken, or baked potatoes.

Optional: 1 tablespoon chopped green olives with the capers. **Yum!!**

DILDO SAUCE OR DRESSING

Yields 1 cup sauce

1/2 cup non-fat plain yogurt
1/2 cup (1% milkfat) cottage cheese
1/2 teaspoon dillweed
1/2 teaspoon black pepper
1/2 teaspoon horseradish
1 teaspoon minced onion
1 teaspoon minced garlic

Whip all ingredients together. Serve with fish, fresh vegetables, or hot vegetables. Also great on baked potatoes. Adjust dill to your liking. Dill and fennel are very distinct flavorings. I like the taste, so I want my dressing to have more dill; but this creamy sauce is great even on a rice cake or cracker.

Chill several hours or overnight.

HORNY MUSTARD DRESSING OR SAUCE

Yields 1 cup

2/3 cup non-fat plain yogurt
1/3 cup reduced-calorie mayonnaise
1 tablespoon Dijon mustard
1 tablespoon honey
1 teaspoon lemon juice

Whip all ingredients together. Chill overnight. Great on vegetables, fruit, lamb, fish, OR ...**yourself!!!** A great facial for a Friday night alone!

FRENCH KISSED DRESSING

Yields 1 cup
Low in calories, high in taste!

1 (8 oz.) can no-salt tomato sauce
2 tablespoons garlic flavored vinegar
1 tablespoon Worcestershire sauce
1 tablespoon minced garlic or fresh garlic
1 tablespoon minced onion or grated fresh onion
1 tablespoon horseradish
Dash of hot pepper seasoning

Optional: 1 teaspoon sugar or 1 package of sugar substitute

Whip all ingredients together. Chill and ....**Wahoo!!!** Good on salad, chicken or your boogers!! Adjust seasonings to taste.

CREAMY ITALIAN DRESSING

Yields 1-1/2 cups

This is not your usual Italian dressing. It contains no oil and can be used as a dip or on baked potatoes.

1 cup (1% milk fat) cottage cheese
1/2 cup non-fat plain yogurt
2-4 cloves garlic, minced
1/2 cup chopped scallions
1 teaspoon black pepper
1 teaspoon basil
1 teaspoon oregano
1 teaspoon thyme
1 teaspoon fresh parsley, chopped

Mix all ingredients together in blender or food processor until very creamy.

Refrigerate several hours. Great as a dip with fresh vegetables. I like it on my baked potatoes, or mixed with tuna fish in a pita pocket.

*SUGGESTION: Add more garlic or a little hot pepper seasoning, or a teaspoon of romano cheese and you can **"zip it up!"***

BLOW ME AWAY BLUE CHEESE DRESSING

Yields 2 cups

In trying to keep the cook's life simple and free to do more productive things with her mate, after you make the Creamy Italian Dressing, add 2-4 ounces of good blue cheese to the above recipe. The whole flavor changes! Double the Italian recipe and cut it in half.   One for the blue cheese and one for the regular Italian. **Two for the price of one!!**

Serve the blue cheese dressing on hearts of lettuce with fresh mushroom slices on top. Very pretty.

SUGGESTION: Take this basic salad dressing one step further and add frozen chopped spinach, drained thoroughly. This combination is fantastic on salmon patties, tuna burgers, or ANY seafood!

Close your eyes and imagine! Creamy consistency, a mild flavor of blue cheese and spinach. It is yummy, and even though it has a little fat, it is SO rich you do not need much.

UNZIP ME DRESSING

Yields 1-1/2 cups

When you hear this name, what do you think of? I think of taking something off and pulling something out!! A sensual name for a sensual vegetable.... CUCUMBERS! Make this dressing slowly... v-e-r-y slowly.

1 **LARGE** cucumber, peeled, seeded and shredded.
   Press with paper towels to remove all excess liquid.
1/2 cup (1% milkfat) cottage cheese
1/2 cup non-fat plain yogurt
   Optional: Use reduced-calorie mayonnaise or low-calorie sour cream.
2 tablespoons fresh chopped parsley
1 tablespoon fresh chopped scallion
1 clove garlic, minced
1 tablespoon black pepper

Blend this concoction until smooth. Do anything you want to with it after that. It is light, delicious, and low-calorie. Very tasty on any vegetable.

COCKTAIL SAUCE

Yields 1 cup

You can't get fancy with cocktail sauce, but the name is too good to leave out of this book.

8 ounces chili sauce
1 tablespoon horseradish
1 clove garlic, finely minced
1 tablespoon lemon juice
1/2 teaspoon Worcestershire sauce
1 tablespoon chopped green onion
Black pepper to taste

Mix together. Change seasonings and chill.

FLAJELLOW

Serves 8

I wanted to have one macaroni salad in this book. Flajellow seems like a good name for this flavorful, moist and tasty recipe.

1 pound (16 ounces) of any variety and flavor of pasta. Tri-color pasta twists look great in this recipe because it is very colorful.
1/2 cup each: pea pods, broccoli, red pepper chunks, radishes, black pitted olives
1 small red onion, sliced into thin rings
1 pint of cherry tomatoes
2 cloves garlic, minced

Dressing:

1/4 cup Dijon mustard
1/4 cup olive oil
1 tablespoon black pepper
2 tablespoons garlic flavored vinegar
1 teaspoon garlic powder or onion powder

Prepare pasta as package directs. Rinse and place in a large bowl. Add the pea pods. If frozen, prepare as package directs. If fresh, clean, remove stems and de-vein. Steam for 3 minutes. Add broccoli, pepper chunks, whole radishes, olives, onion, garlic and cherry tomatoes. Toss to mix thoroughly. In a covered container, mix the dressing and pour over salad. Cover and refrigerate for several hours. Toss occasionally. **Beautiful and delicious.**

Note: If using spinach pasta, you may want to use more radish slices or black olives for color. If using plain color pasta, adjust color of vegetables to your liking. I am very visual. I think color, appeal, and flavor are equally important.

START USING TRI-COLOR PASTA. It makes dishes so interesting and people tend to think it was harder to make and much more unique!

CHEW ME

Serves 6-8

This is a crunchy coleslaw that is easy to make and very low in calories. <u>Chew away!</u>

1 medium head of cabbage; or 1 small head of green cabbage, and 1 small head of
  red cabbage (I like to use both kinds of cabbage in my coleslaw. It's pretty.)
2 carrots, shredded
2 stalks celery, chopped
1 medium onion, chopped
1 clove garlic, minced
1 red pepper - cut, seeded, and chopped

Dressing:

1/2 cup low-calorie creamy Italian dressing
1/4 cup reduced-calorie mayonnaise
1/4 cup plain non-fat yogurt
1 teaspoon garlic powder
1 tablespoon black pepper
1 tablespoon red wine vinegar
1 teaspoon dry mustard
1 teaspoon chopped pimento
1 teaspoon sugar or sugar substitute

Optional: raisins, black olives, or egg whites, shredded

All of the above ingredients can be changed to suit your taste. This is a very general
coleslaw recipe, but very tasty.

Shred cabbage both ways: long strips and short shreds. Again, it looks very interesting
when you use 2 colors and shred them in <u>BOTH</u> long and short pieces.

Combine all vegetables. Toss with dressing. Chill and serve in a pretty bowl. Top with
shredded egg whites, chopped olives, pepperocinis, parsley, or raisins.

STRADDLE ME SALAD

Serves 4

This salad can be used as a main dish, because it is a curried chicken salad that is loaded with taste and body.

4 cups mixed greens - Spinach, Iceberg Lettuce, or Romaine. Again, variety makes every dish look so much more impressive and the best part is, you didn't have to do much extra work!!

2 cups cooked cut-up chicken in large chunks
1 large orange, cut into sections, or use mandarin oranges, drained
1 large banana, cut into slices and dipped in lemon juice
1/2 cup golden raisins
1/2 cup chopped walnuts, no-salt peanuts, cashews, or sunflower seeds

Optional: shredded coconut - (Coconut is sweet and delicious in this salad).

Dressing:

4 ounces non-fat or low-fat orange yogurt
1/2 cup low-calorie mayonnaise, or reduced-calorie salad dressing
1 tablespoon curry powder - adjust to suit your taste. I like curry.

Line a large bowl with salad greens. Add chicken, orange sections and bananas. Mix in raisins and nuts. Cover with plastic wrap. Chill. Before serving, mix mayonnaise, yogurt, and curry powder. Pour over top of salad or pass around.

If you have pineapples in your area, try to get the boats that are left after the pineapple has been removed. My supermarket will save me the shells when they take out the fruit. (Call ahead). Or, you can do it yourself. **This is great in a pineapple boat!**

Note: For the adventurous, go for a coconut! I cannot begin to tell you how to "bang the shit" out of this rock hard ball, but it is gorgeous when this chicken salad is served in it!

SUGGESTION: Substitute large shrimp, lobster, crab, turkey or ham chunks for chicken. It's the fruit and nuts with the curry dressing that makes this so tasty. I've given you enough for this recipe. You aren't paying this much for the book!!

SHAKE IT BABY SALAD

Serves 4-6

What would a health cookbook be like without that iron rich green called "spinach"? The only problem I have with spinach is that I wish someone would invent a way to get all the sand out! Nothing turns me off more than grit in my spinach. Wash it thoroughly in your sink and then run it under the faucet again in a colander. **Drain and press dry with paper towels.**

1 package fresh spinach, well washed
1 cup fresh mushroom slices
1 small red onion, thinly sliced
1 clove garlic, mashed
1 tablespoon black pepper

Optional: 1 tablespoon small capers or black olive slices

Dressing:

1/4 cup olive oil
1 tablespoon fresh lemon juice
1 teaspoon red wine vinegar
1/2 cup hard-boiled egg whites, grated (about 3-4 eggs)

In a large bowl, place mashed garlic and then mash again. (For those who like garlic, chop some extra and serve on the side.) Place spinach in bowl. Add mushrooms, onions and pepper. Toss. Pour on dressing. Sprinkle with egg whites.

Note: To make a Dijon dressing, add 1 tablespoon of Dijon mustard to olive oil and vinegar mixture.

SUGGESTION: If you do not have any problem with salt retention, then layer the top with anchovies. Artichoke hearts are also great!

You cannot go wrong with a basic spinach salad, **but you can be as creative as you like.**

Any of my dressings can be used over this salad, but I do not want to take away from the lightness of it, so I stay with a simple vinaigrette dressing. As always, I am a garlic fanatic and use more than most people.

<u>**Mrs. Boner likes spinach and uses it as a base for many salads.**</u>

GREEK SALAD FROM BEHIND

Serves 8-12

There are two things you have to do when you make a Greek salad: First you have to play your music very loud; and second, you have to dance wildly.

It is not a low-calorie salad and is loaded with sodium. But, if it is going to be most of your dinner or your entire lunch, then you can get away with it. At least I wanted you to have a delicious recipe in case you did not know what really makes it up... feta cheese, black olives (Greek style from deli) and anchovies. Oh! So Good! **Great when you have PMS and need something to blame your water retention on! Use anchovies, - they can't talk back!**

Ingredients:

Several heads of lettuce torn into small pieces - Iceberg, Curly Endive, and Romaine
3 large tomatoes, washed and cut into medium chunks
8 ounces (about 1 cup) part-skim feta cheese. Cut in cubes, if possible.
1/2 cup Greek olives; or 1 can large black olives marinated in olive oil and garlic
      overnight.
1/2 cup sliced green onion
1 can anchovy fillets, drained thoroughly. I like to use the flat ones for this recipe.

Dressing to be made the night before:

2/3 cup olive oil
Several garlic cloves, crushed
1/4 cup wine vinegar
1/2 teaspoon black pepper
1/2 teaspoon oregano

Combine all the dressing ingredients in a jar with a lid. Mix several times until everything is well blended. Refrigerate overnight and allow to come to room temperature 2 hours before using. Remove garlic, if desired.

Using a large bowl or serving platter, which I like to use, assemble all the above ingredients in your most "artistic" fashion. Pour dressing over all. **Dive in and drink your hearts out for the rest of the night!**

continued on next page...

SUGGESTION: This salad is great with garlic bread, chicken, and Fuzzy Navel Dessert. Many people use potato salad in this recipe. You can mound your potato salad under the lettuce and it becomes quite a surprise! You can also stuff tomato shells with potato salad and surround it on a bed of lettuce with cheese, olives, and anchovies... a very unique lunch dish.

Note: I do crave Greek salad on occasion. I like the feta and anchovies. I have an appreciation for the art of Greek cooking. HAIL TO ZORBA!

Suggested Meals:

For Lunch:
           Bangers
           Greek Salad From Behind
           Garlic Bread
           Golden Ram

For Dinner
With Chicken:
           Greek Salad From Behind
           Horny Hens
           Spotted Dick
           Fuzzy Navels

For Dinner
With Fish:
           Jizz Wizz
           Greek Salad From Behind
           Sensuous Snapper
           Wet Dreams

TM

HOT-FLASHIN' ANTIPASTO

Serves a Gang!

I like antipasto. Sure it's got cheese, cold cuts, oil, and anchovies, which if you put them all together, spells fat, trouble, and more fat! But, I will have it just by itself for dinner, so I feel that it has protein, vegetables, and is really a very well-balanced meal.

I do, however, have one very large problem when I eat it out and I'm with my husband or other people. I do not care how many people you order for; when it comes time to "divvy" up the ingredients, I am always feeling guilty because I gave something away to someone else that I wanted! It's like a divorce. One for you... one for me... do you want this? I can have that. I hate it! I want my own and I want a lot! I do not do sharing well! This recipe has only one requirement... **A LARGE PLATTER! A HUGE PLATTER!** It is going to have everything on it for a main meal or full appetizer portion for 8-10 people.

IT'S THE ONLY WAY TO FLY!! HERE GOES... LOTS OF INGREDIENTS... LITTLE WORK... YOU CREATE WHERE YOU WANT EVERYTHING TO GO!

Marinate all the ingredients below several hours beforehand in a low-calorie Italian dressing.

Small button mushrooms, drained - (jar)
Small whole beets, drained - (jar)
Chick peas (15-1/2 oz. can) washed and drained
Artichoke hearts, drained

It looks very interesting if you want to marinate and assemble them altogether, but in case some people do not like all the ingredients, it might be safer to do them in separate containers.

Three types of lettuce: Bibb, Romaine, Curly Endive. Again, it looks so unique when you change from the everyday look. The color is incredible and it was no more work than if you used only one kind.

Olive oil and Balsamic vinegar - or any flavor vinegar of your choice. Serve on the side. Do NOT pour over.

continued on next page...

Miscellaneous Ingredients -

HERE GOES......

Red, green, and yellow peppers, washed and cut into 1/2 inch strips
Cherry tomatoes
Hard-boiled egg white halves only (stuff with small capers or caviar).
    Do not use yolks to devil.
Scallions - keep them long. Don't chop.
Whole pimentos, drained - (jar)

1 (15-1/2 oz.) can of water-packed tuna, drained. Leave in a large chunk. Salmon, sardines, or a seafood blend can also be used. Anchovies are optional, but so good. A large portion of a fish looks interesting, and for the people who do not want coldcuts (meat), it's appropriate.

Lemon wedges
Yellow and green zucchini strips
Radishes, carrots and celery strips
Broccoli, Cauliflower, or Brussels Sprouts

SUGGESTED CHEESES: Mozzarella, provolone, fontina, or Lorraine Swiss - cut into strips. Low-fat cheese, please.

SUGGESTED MEATS: Assorted turkey coldcuts; i.e. turkey ham, turkey salami, turkey pastrami, etc. There is a high sodium content, but a lot less fat.

Wrap a cold cut around the cheese sticks, zucchini strips, or carrots and celery.

Fasten with a curly tipped toothpick. **ASSEMBLE ANY WAY YOU LIKE!**

I think that with a good loaf of bread, bread sticks, pita or bagel chips, your guests will not have any trouble getting what they want and you'll get EXACTLY what you deserve!

THIS ONE IS GOOD!!

SUGGESTION: If using frozen Brussels sprouts (I use them all the time), do not cook. Let them defrost and marinate them. One of MY favorites!

Note: If YOU can think of anything else to put on this platter or any other delicacies, go for it! I'm too pooped thinking of all the ingredients you can use!

CROTCH CALAMARI - SQUID

Serves 4-6

As an appetizer, it is beautiful on your antipasto platter. As a main salad, it is perfect stuffed in tomato cups and garnished with lemon wedges and deviled eggs.

This is also a basic marinade for ceviche! If you do not want to go through the work of cutting and boiling the squid, you can use any fish you like.

1 1/2 - 2 pounds calamari. Have your **seaman** (another one of those "good" words!) wash them well and prepare them the best he can. They are not the big octopus you think they are. They are small and easy to prepare, and... <u>VERY</u> tasty!!

1/2 cup olive oil
Juice of 1 lemon
1 medium sweet onion, diced
4 cloves garlic, minced
1/4 cup chopped parsley
1/4 teaspoon crushed red pepper
2 tablespoons wine vinegar
1 teaspoon basil
1 teaspoon black pepper
1/2 cup white wine - optional

After you have cleaned the squid, cut, dice or prepare in strips. Place in boiling water approximately 5 minutes, depending on the size of the squid. (Do not over cook, as the squid will become tough). When done, plunge into cold water. Mix squid with all the other ingredients and chill. Marinate overnight, stirring occasionally.

It's a real trip to eat this. I love it and I don't mind a taste of the exotic.

<u>SUBSTITUTIONS FOR SQUID:</u> Mussels, oysters, scallops, shrimp, crab, seafood blend, whitefish, or any fish that you do not have to do a lot of preparation before, or that can be served without any cooking.

Note: This is a basic marinade and is easy for any salad. Add extra onion, garlic or even green pepper, diced.

Suggestions for serving: Antipasto platter, side salad in tomato cups, in hoagie rolls with tomato and shredded lettuce, or in pita pockets.

GAR LICK ME DRESSING

Yields 1-1/2 cups

1/2 cup olive oil
1/2 cup chicken bouillon - no salt kind
1/4 cup red wine vinegar or garlic flavored vinegar
4 cloves garlic, minced very fine
Juice of 1/2 fresh squeezed lemon
1 tablespoon Dijon or spicy brown mustard
1/2 tablespoon fresh black pepper
1/2 teaspoon sugar substitute

Mix all ingredients in blender or covered container. Refrigerate overnight. Bring to room temperature two hours before serving. **It's great!** I use this basic dressing for marinating chicken, over hot broccoli or cauliflower, or I add more garlic and eat it with a spoon when I want to keep people away.

Note: One spoonful before a date and he'll never ask you out again!! A very polite way of saying to your date, "I'm sorry. It must have been something I ate!" **He will never call again!**

TY-ME-UP DRESSING

Yields 2/3 cup

1/2 cup olive oil
2 tablespoons red wine vinegar
2 tablespoons fresh chopped thyme leaves or dried thyme
1 tablespoon fresh snipped parsley
1 tablespoon fresh lemon juice
1 clove garlic, minced
1/2 teaspoon black pepper
1 tablespoon fresh green onion, chopped

This dressing is very good on lamb, chicken, veal, or salads. Mix all ingredients in a covered container. Adjust herbs, but you do want a colorful and tasty dressing. Good on a plain salad, or on tomato slices and egg wedges, asparagus and hearts of palm, and spinach and fresh mushrooms.

NOTE: Mrs. Boner will give you a hint: a secret from the depths of my most inner food fantasies.... to make almost any liquid dressing like the ones above, a whiter and thicker sauce, get rid of the liquid and substitute 1/2 cup non-fat plain yogurt, 1/2 cup low-fat cottage cheese, and stir. Use the same dry ingredients like the herbs, mustard and even the lemon juice. Just make it thick instead of thin. You can use for dips too! Make more than you need and store in Mason jars. They keep for a week. IN FACT THEY ARE LIKE YOUR AUTHOR: THEY GET BETTER WITH AGE. USE ME!

POOP DU JOUR

Serves 8

The poop comes from this Mexican spicy salad that can be enhanced by adding as much Pumpin' Picante and jalapenos as you want.

8 tortillas or 8 pita bread slices split. Or, split a baked potato in half and use it as your base for this recipe. For any recipe that calls for bread, rice or any other starch, I use baked potatoes.

1 pound ground turkey, sliced chicken breasts, or ground beef
1 medium onion, chopped
2 cloves garlic, minced
1 jalapeno - cut in half, seeded, and chopped
1 tablespoon chili powder
1 teaspoon cumin seed
1 8 oz. can red kidney beans, drained
1 large tomato, diced
1 medium head lettuce, shredded
2-4 ounces shredded low-fat Cheddar or Monterey jack cheese
Pumpin' Picante/Holey Guacamole... see index

If using tortillas, fry in a small amount of oil until brown and keep warm in the oven covered in foil. You can spray a baking sheet with non-stick cooking spray and press the tortilla down to coat. Bake in a 325 degree oven until brown. If using pitas, bake until warm.

In a large frying pan, brown meat with onion, garlic, jalapeno, and seasonings. When browned, drain off fat. Add kidney beans and heat through.

Remove tortillas and start layering: Meat mixture, tomato, shredded lettuce, and cheese. Serve with extra nacho slices and above sauces.

*Note: If you want a seafood Poop du Jour use shrimp. Play with this salad. Any combination of ingredients will work. For people who like a special light dinner, **this is fun and easy**. People can assemble their own tortilla as they would a pizza. Make a group game....*

Margharitas, Nasty Nachos, Pumpin' Picante, Holey Guacamole, Poop du Jour, Fuzzy Navels, Chocolate Orgasm

SEIZE ME SALAD

Serves 8

Seize me to say the least! This updated version of (yes! you guessed it) Caesar Salad, is definitely foreplay! Your mouth will wake up and your body will respond to these incredible flavors. **If he does not seize you, then seize him! The rest is history!**

My best Olive Oil Marinade:

1/2 cup olive oil
4 cloves of garlic, crushed

Add garlic to oil in cruet. Allow to blend several hours. This is also the oil I put in a spray bottle and use for all my recipes. Keeping oil in a spray (mister) bottle is a very easy way to lightly spray oil on your foods.

Salad Ingredients:

2 bunches Romaine Lettuce
1 head Boston Lettuce
3/4 cup grated parmesan cheese
1/2 teaspoon dry mustard
1/2 teaspoon black pepper
Juice of 2 lemons - about 1/4 cup
1 egg, plus 1 egg white
Dash Worcestershire sauce
1 can anchovy fillets - drained on paper towels
Homemade croutons *

Prepare Salad:

In large salad bowl, add 1 tablespoon garlic oil, 2-3 anchovies and Worcestershire sauce. Mash all together and make a paste. Add mustard, pepper and lemon juice. Beat eggs. Add all greens and toss. Add egg mixture and toss again. Add parmesan and extra anchovies. Top with croutons and remaining oil. Mix a few times. That's it folks! If you do not want to get fancy, toss everything anyway you want and add the croutons last. There are so many great flavors and varieties to this salad.

* Homemade croutons: Cut Italian bread into 1/2 inch slices. Spread on baking sheet which is lightly sprayed with olive oil, and bake at 325 degrees for 20 minutes - until golden brown. Spray top of slices with a little oil if you like. **Remember to bake slowly so the bread gets golden brown and does not burn.** Remove from oven and allow to cool. Cut slices into cubes and toss in your salad.

SUGGESTIONS: Instead of plain lettuce, use, Iceberg, spinach, or endive. Usually you get Caesar salad with just Romaine. Why? Using several greens is unique and colorful. Remember, we are trying to teach imagination in this book. You are gifted and unique. Let these little tricks prove it!

TONGUED TUNA

Serves 4

This is a <u>great</u> salad that can also be changed for variety. It is low-fat, low-calorie and rich in protein and carbohydrate power for that "quickie" you may need in the afternoon! **Instead of falling asleep at your desk after lunch, you will be chasing that special someone around it!**

2 (6-1/2 oz.) or 1 (15-1/2 oz.) can of water-packed tuna. Rinse in a colander to remove excess salt. Salt free tuna is bland, boring and more expensive.

<u>Combine in a large bowl:</u>

2 large scallions, chopped; or 1 small white onion, chopped fine.
1 stalk celery, chopped
1/3 cup green or red pepper, chopped (use both - it looks pretty)
1 tablespoon chopped parsley
Juice of one lemon
Pepper to taste

<u>Stir in one of the following:</u>

1 cup chick peas or garbanzo beans
1 cup peas
1 cup green beans

Note: You can use frozen vegetables for this salad

<u>Mix:</u>

1/2 cup non-fat plain yogurt
1 tablespoon mustard
1/2 teaspoon horseradish
Dill, rosemary or curry powder - any of these will add flavor

Toss altogether. Serve in tomato cups or in green pepper shells. Garnish with cucumbers, radishes, celery sticks, and assorted whole wheat crackers.

Note: I like tuna salad drier, rather than creamy. Add additional lo-cal Italian, creamy garlic, or any other liquid to moisten. I stay away from mayonnaise and heavy salad dressings because they have a very high fat content. Once you get used to lighter eating and tasting the food in a more natural vein, you will automatically reduce your use of these condiments. **You really get hooked on lighter fare.**

Entrees
(Main Event!)

FETTISH FETTICINI

Serves 6-8

I named this recipe Fettish Fetticini because I am going to keep it simple, low-calorie and open for suggestions! But, you can spice it up with many other ingredients and make it YOUR favorite dish. <u>Whatever your "fettish", this is the dish!</u>

1 (16 oz.) package of FETTICINI pasta
1/2 cup (1% milk fat) cottage cheese
1/2 cup non-fat plain yogurt, or lite sour cream
2 tablespoons butter substitute - dry (do not mix with water)
1 tablespoon fresh minced garlic or garlic powder
2 tablespoons fresh parsley (1 tablespoon for recipe, 1 tablespoon for garnish)
1/2 cup grated parmesan cheese
Black pepper to taste
1/4 cup skim milk, (if noodle mixture looks too dry)
1 teaspoon olive oil

Garnish: cherry tomatoes

Prepare FETTICINI as package directs, adding 1 teaspoon of olive oil to the water to prevent boil-over onto stove. While pasta is cooking, mix all the other ingredients in a separate bowl. Reserve some extra parsley, black pepper, and cherry tomatoes for garnish.

Drain pasta. Leave small amount (1/4 cup) of water in pot with pasta. Add the other ingredients. Stir thoroughly and add the extra milk if too thick. As the pasta cools, it gets harder, so <u>stir while mixture is very hot.</u>

<u>NOW FOR THE</u> **<u>FETTISH</u>:**

In 1/4 cup olive oil or 2-3 tablespoons butter or margarine, saute' 1/2 pound of sliced mushrooms with fresh garlic and chopped onions. Add this mixture to the pasta.

Saute' chicken, shrimp, crab, tuna, scallops, prosciutto, broccoli, peas, zucchini... <u>ANYTHING!</u> Play with this. Season heavily and saute' any ingredients you want when you toss this dish together. **Your friends will think it is fantastic!** Serve on a large pretty platter. Add garnish and enjoy!

SUGGESTION: You can add 1 teaspoon olive oil to pasta after it has been drained. It is not a lot of fat and the little extra flavor goes a long way. I prefer olive oil over the milk to keep it moist, but the milk is the best way to keep the fat content lower.

Note: Any pasta can be used... noodles, linguini, shells - whole wheat or spinach.

<u>Suggested Meal</u>:　　　　　Butt Holes
　　　　　　　　　　　　　　Shake It Baby Salad
　　　　　　　　　　　　　　Fettish Fetticini
　　　　　　　　　　　　　　Bloomer Pudding

GET HUNG (SCHLONG) SAUSAGE

Serves 4-8

I don't like eating processed food! In any form! Especially meats! They are high in fat and sodium. But once in a while when you pass the meat counter and look at those delightfully long and colorful yummy sausages, don't you wet your lips? Just a little? **Well, I do!!** For those occasions when you've just got to have A BIG ONE in your mouth, this recipe is perfect! Keep it long or cut it up into pieces. Only **you** know what **you** like and what **you** can handle.

This dish takes 15-30 minutes to prepare and is very economical and tasty. Everything gets done at the same time and you can't blow it. It's colorful AND delicious!

Ingredients:

1 (8-16) oz. package of your favorite spaghetti. (Prepare as package directs.) 2 ounces
    dry pasta per serving.
1 to 2 pounds of good Italian sausage, uncooked - sweet or hot; or 8 all-beef knockwurst;
    or 8-12 all-beef frankfurters; or any all-beef sausage you prefer. I also like Polish
    Kielbasa. It's tasty and doesn't require much cooking. I'll be using sausage.

2 tablespoons olive oil plus 2 tablespoons water
1 large green pepper, seeded and cut into 1/2 inch strips
2 large onions, sliced thin
4-6 cloves garlic, minced well
Pepper, oregano, basil, thyme, etc., to taste
2 cups Marquis De Sade's Marinara Sauce, or your own tomato sauce.

Optional: parmesan cheese, red wine or Marsala

Cooking times for meats:

Uncooked sausage: cook according to the variety and quantity of meat - usually 30
    minutes or longer.
Pre-cooked Italian Sausage: 15-20 minutes
Knockwurst: 10-15 minutes
Hot Dogs: 5-10 minutes

Prick (I love that word) each uncooked sausage with a fork once, to drain excess fats during cooking. In a large frying pan, in 1 inch of boiling water, simmer the sausages approximately 30 minutes until thoroughly cooked and most fat has been cooked out.

continued on next page...

While sausage is cooking, in another large frying pan, heat olive oil and water. Add all remaining ingredients except spaghetti and sauce. Saute' over medium heat about 10 minutes or until vegetables are tender. Change the seasonings to suit your taste. I like things spicy and hot so I always add more garlic and pepper. Simmer on low heat to keep hot until ready to serve.

Now everything is cooking and you are "hot" for this dish! Prepare pasta according to package directions. Add a little olive oil to your pasta water. You won't get any boil-over. The oil keeps the starch under it and can't over-boil onto your stove.

Drain pasta. Heat the tomato sauce and stir into vegetables. Add drained sausages. Place on a large platter. Add fresh romano and extra chopped garlic. Serve more sauce on the side. You may add red cooking wine or Marsala to the vegetables.

Note: This dish can also be used in hoagie rolls. It makes a hot sausage submarine sandwich. If you do not want to use the marinara sauce in this book, you can use one that is not of a meat base.

SUGGESTIONS: In the diet section of your supermarket or under gourmet foods, you can find artichoke, whole wheat and spinach pastas. They are very nutritious and do have a slightly different taste and consistency. Artichoke pasta is made from the Jerusalem artichoke so it is a vegetable-based pasta. Whole wheat has to be treated with respect as it has a mind and body of its own. I think this recipe is best with plain pasta.

Suggested Meal: Bangers
                        Seize Me Salad
                        Get Hung (Schlong) Sausage
                        Wet Dreams

HORNY HENS

1 Hen per person - Serves 4

These babies turn themselves **on!** How come when we go out to dinner and order these "midget" chickens, they look so elegant? Or, if we are served them at a banquet or at someone's home for a dinner party, we feel so impressed and exclaim to the hostess: "Oh, you shouldn't have fussed so much!" Well, get **REAL** people! Hens are over-priced in restaurants. They are easy to fix, inexpensive, and can be made up ahead of time. Let them think you fussed! Go on... do it! Hens are impressive and yummy. They look beautiful and are also great for lunch the next day.

Ingredients:

4 Cornish game hens - about 1 pound each, cleaned and ready for fixin'
1 jar apricot preserves, low-calorie variety

Seasonings:

Ginger - as much as you like
Garlic powder
Pepper
Lite soy sauce

Preheat oven to 350 degrees. Cornish hens take 60 minutes to make.

Line a shallow roasting pan with foil. Place the hens in the pan and roast uncovered for 30 minutes. Remove from oven. Mix all the other ingredients together and baste the hens. Return to oven for another 15 minutes. Remove from oven. Baste again. I baste during the last 30 minutes because I do not like burnt skin. You should remove the skin before you eat the hens, but, what the hey! The seasonings do penetrate the skin and for this dish, why NOT leave the skin on to roast and take it off later! Serve with additional preserves on the side.

Remember to baste twice - 15 minutes apart. This really does enhance the flavor of the bird. Add a little extra ginger, soy sauce, or garlic powder.

Note: I like sweet and sour flavors, but do not like the calories or the sugar in them. There is no fat in preserves, but they do contain fructose. So, DO use low-calorie jellies. Add a few more spices, and you'll see how rich they taste.

SUBSTITUTIONS FOR HENS: Chicken, turkey breast - sliced and ready to eat, or turkey burgers.

SUBSTITUTIONS FOR APRICOT PRESERVES: Low-calorie orange marmalade, peach preserves, sweet and sour sauce, pineapple preserves.

Suggested Meal: Smegma Surprise
                               Mixed Green Salad (to be announced in second book, and it
                                                   will be "mixed")
                               Horny Hens
                               Polynesian Pea Pea Pods
                               Taste My Cumquats

FINGER LICKIN' LAMB CHOPS WITH BREATH MINT JELLY

Serves 4

A delicious dish! Here's a helpful suggestion: while opening the jar of mint jelly, just breath hard or groan. **That's how the breath gets in there!!**

2 (1 inch) loin or rib chops per serving
1 shoulder chop or lamb steak per serving

(I am going to use rib chops)

8 (1 inch thick rib chops)
Juice of 2 lemons
4 cloves fresh garlic, minced
1 teaspoon thyme
1 teaspoon basil
1 teaspoon oregano
1 teaspoon rosemary
Black pepper

Note: All herbs can be changed to suit your taste

Mix all the ingredients together. Press mixture on both sides of the chops and place in a large baking pan. Marinate the chops 3-4 hours before serving. Turn every hour to thoroughly blend the flavors. Keep under refrigeration when marinating. Remove 30 minutes before broiling and allow the chops to come to room temperature.

Broil 3 inches from heat for 5-7 minutes on each side. Lamb, in my opinion, should be cooked like steak... well, medium or rare.

Serve with lemon wedges, parsley sprigs and "breath mint jelly." I like to dip lamb chops in horseradish and mustard, also.

SUGGESTION: The same marinating ingredients for the lamb can be used on chicken, Cornish hens, or fish. If broiling, the coating gets very crispy; if baking, it's just plain delicious!

Note: "Breath mint jelly" can be obtained at your local supermarket. After eating this sumptuous dish, get yourself some exercise. Walk and buy ANOTHER jar, so you'll have it on hand! Or, if you can think of some other exercise... GO FOR IT!

Suggested Meal: Hot Lips/Hot Hips
                         Cock Rings
                         Finger Lickin' Lambchops
                         with Breath Mint Jelly
                         The Crown Jewels
                         Taste My Cumquats

WET PANTY PRIMAVERA

Serves 4-6

Fresh and moist. That's the name of the game, and this pasta is guaranteed to do the same!

1 (16 oz.) package of your favorite pasta. I like linquini for this one - artichoke, whole wheat, or enriched is OK.

Here we go. Basic ingredients to saute' your favorite vegetables:

1/4 cup olive oil
1 tablespoon butter
1/2 cup chopped onion
4-6 cloves garlic, minced
1/4 cup chopped fresh parsley
Black pepper to taste (I like lots of pepper)
1 tablespoon mixed Italian seasonings (thyme, basil, oregano)
4 cups (approximately) of miscellaneous vegetables, such as: broccoli, zucchini, mushrooms, green and red peppers, snow peas, baby carrots, green beans, asparagus, etc.
1/2 cup parmesan cheese, grated

Note: I do not like to use more than three vegetables for this dish. I used broccoli, mushrooms and zucchini.

Cut all vegetables into flowerets or 1/2 inch slices. In a large frying pan, saute' vegetables in olive oil and butter. Add onion, garlic, parsley and herbs. Cook for 5-8 minutes. Stir occasionally. Use a wok for a crunchier texture. Add more water if necessary.

Prepare pasta as package directs. Drain. Add an extra teaspoon of olive oil to pasta and toss with the vegetable mixture.

Adjust seasonings and serve with parmesan cheese.

If you are using frozen vegetables, cook as the package directs and just saute' the onions and garlic. Cook vegetables to the texture you want, depending on how much you use. Again, variety and flavor makes this dish easy and appealing to everyone.

continued on next page...

SUGGESTION: Use one (4 or 8 oz.) can no-salt tomato sauce to make a red sauce, and for a moister dish, add a little water. Some vegetables contain more water, so the liquid you add may vary, depending on what vegetable you use.

Note: I give you the most nutritious and simple recipes I know, but you are the chef and you can adjust any recipe to your liking. **That's why cooking is fun! You are in control and you do what YOU want to do!** *Usually, 1 cup of vegetables is enough for 1 serving.   If you use a pasta dish like this with your dinner, you can cut back on the amount of vegetables because you have other things to eat. If you are serving this dish by itself, you may want to add an extra cup or two of vegetables to your recipe.*

Suggested Meal: Nipple Nuggets
                         Seize Me Salad
                         Wet Panty Primavera
                         Spermoni

COCK AU VIN

Serves 8

My version of the "tickler". A French Classic. Mine, however, has more substance and "cock" to it. I want to make this recipe for 8. It is very difficult to get 2 chickens or 8 large pieces of chicken in a Dutch oven without making yourself crazy in the process of rearranging everything. So, I do most of my chicken entrees in the oven and bake.

2 (2-1/2 to 3 pound) chickens, cut up; or 8 large chicken breasts; or enough chicken in any combination of parts you like. Half chickens do well and can be served very easily. Remove skin if you prefer. For most of my recipes, you'll note that I remove the skin.

16 small whole white onions, peeled and left whole
1 pound of large mushroom caps and stems, washed and separated into large pieces
8 carrots, pared and cut into 1 inch pieces
Garlic cloves - whole and as much as you like
1 cup (chicken) bouillon. Use the low-salt kind. Dissolve 2 packages in 1 cup of water.
1 cup red Burgundy wine
1 tablespoon pepper - more if you prefer
2 bay leaves
1 tablespoon thyme
1 tablespoon fresh parsley, chopped

Optional: Celery... stalks, cut into 1 inch pieces

Preheat oven to 400 degrees

Note: **Since I do not cook with salt, I have to rely on garlic, onions, and celery.** For this recipe you can use as many vegetables as you like. Several stalks of celery will add flavor and color. The flavor also comes from the Burgundy blending with the other ingredients.

Line a large broiler pan or roasting pan with foil twice. Spread chicken evenly in pan. Mix all the other ingredients and pour over the chicken. Bake, uncovered for 30 minutes. Remove from oven and baste. Return to oven for another 15 minutes. Remove and baste again. During the final 15 minutes of cooking, make sure the vegetables are not too brown, but still done. Cover if necessary during the final few minutes.

continued on next page...

*te: I like to cover this dish and let it stay in the oven for an additional half hour after
 oven has been turned off. The flavors blend and when ready to serve, it is still very
t and tender. You can NOT ruin dishes like this!!

ne hour is sufficient for this dish, but do baste 2 times. Oven temperatures vary and
metimes you have to just "eyeball" things. I think covering a recipe like this insures
at it won't get dried out, especially if you do not have the fat on the chicken. But for
is recipe, you can always remove the fat and you still will have a delicious sauce and
getable medley to spoon over your chicken. Serve extra juice on the side.

<u>uggested Meal:</u>

Blue Balls
Seize Me Salad
Cock Au Vin
Pussy Potatoes
Twatty's Torte

CHILI COME ON ME

Serves 6-8

When it's "cold" outside and you want to get "hot" inside, what could be better than a bowl of chili made with ground turkey or vegetarian style? It's a GREAT way to serve a group, or as a main dish for **YOUR** favorite "dish". **With bread and salad, you have a nutritious and inexpensive meal that can be prepared in advance, so you have more time for** YOUR **hot night ahead!**

1 1/2 pounds ground turkey/or any good ground beef
2 medium onions, chopped
1 small green pepper - washed, seeded, and chopped
4 cloves garlic, minced
2 pickled jalapenos, rinsed and chopped. You can use a fresh jalapeno, but I like the
    pickled ones better for this recipe.
2 tablespoons chili seasoning
1/2 teaspoon crushed red pepper
1 teaspoon cumin
1 (15 1/2 oz.) can pinto beans or red kidney beans, drained
1 (12 oz.) can tomato paste
1 1/2 cups water

Garnish with 1 cup shredded low-fat Cheddar or Monterey jack cheese, and 1/4 cup green onions (scallions), chopped.

In a hot skillet, brown the ground turkey. Drain off the fat. In a Dutch oven or large kettle, add the turkey to all the other ingredients. Cover and simmer for 1 to 1-1/2 hours, stirring occasionally. You can add the beans during the last 30 minutes, but I like to add them altogether to get the chili real soft and gooey. Just before serving, top with cheese and green onions.

Note: If chili gets too thick, add a little water. Alter the ingredients to suit your taste.... more onion, pepper, garlic, jalapenos, etc. Let cool. Refrigerate or freeze.

<u>Suggested Meal:</u>   Whoretilla Chips
                            Holey Guacamole
                            Pumpin' Picante
                            Shake It Baby Salad
                            Chili Come On Me
                            Bread
                            Douche Delight

FORE-SKINNED CHICKEN

Serves 6-8

could have easily written a "dirty" chicken, or a "fowl-mouthed" poultry cookbook. I eat chicken almost every day. My husband could cluck, shed feathers and would lay eggs, if he had to!! But, in this book I wanted to give you a variety of recipes, so I only used four chicken dishes. One is Oriental, one is French, and this one is Mexican... OLE'! The last is Italian. This Mexican recipe is very seasoned and easy to prepare.

2 (2-1/2 to 3 pound) chickens cut up; or 8 large chicken breasts.

Wash the chicken good. Make sure for this recipe the skin is off. It is not difficult to remove the skin from the chicken. **Just pretend it is someone you despise and start pulling! In no time, you will break into a sweat, swear all sorts of obscenities at the chicken, and then the task will be completed!**

4 large onions, peeled and cut into slices
2-4 green and red peppers - washed, seeded, and cut into strips
Garlic cloves.. all you want - 100 cloves is perfect! (just kidding!)
2 jalapeno peppers - seeded, cut and diced
1 teaspoon each of cumin seed, black pepper, parsley, and chile seasoning
1 can tomatoes and green chilies
1 can stewed tomatoes, no-salt variety preferred
1/2 cup lower-calorie, reduced-fat, shredded Monterey jack cheese

Garnish: Several pepperocinis or pickled jalapenos (any variety from a jar)

Preheat oven to 400 degrees

Line a large roasting pan with foil twice. It saves clean-up. Place all the chicken in the pan. Spread vegetables, seasonings, and all the other ingredients, except cheese, over chicken. Adjust seasonings to suit your taste. Bake, uncovered, for 30 minutes. Remove from oven and baste. Place back in oven for an additional 30 minutes. Remove from oven. Sprinkle with cheese. Cover with foil and allow to cool several minutes before serving. On a large platter, garnish chicken with peppers and additional parsley.

What could be simpler than this! Serve with Beans and Rice, Ice Cream and/or Sherbert. **AND THEN.... Ole' me!** (Oh-Lay-Me) !

Suggested Meal: **MEXICAN FIESTA**

Whoretilla Chips
Holey Guacamole
Pumpin' Picante
Fore-Skinned Chicken
Down & Dirty Rice
Poopy Pintos
Golden Ram

CHICKEN SCALLOPENIS

Serves 6-8

If you think I'm going to give you a Scallopenis like you have eaten before, forget it! This is my Italian Chicken Dish - the only one of hundreds I can give you. (My next book will have many more). **It's going to be great,** loaded, and aimed to please! Please note the words "aimed and loaded". This stuff is not easy to write folks! I'm doing this all alone!!

If you think that I'm going to give you a flattened piece of chicken, that's also wrong. You are going to get a REAL penis, not a fake one... a LARGE portion, not a sample!

4-6 large chicken breasts, skinned; or 2 (2-1/2 to 3 pound) chickens, cut-up; or 4 half chickens.

Note: I use half chickens for this recipe. It is easy to get the skin off and easy to serve and garnish.

In a VERY large bowl, combine the following:

4 large onions, sliced
4 cloves garlic, minced
6 Italian plum tomatoes, washed and sliced
1/2 pound fresh mushrooms, sliced
2 green peppers - washed, seeded and cut into strips
2 red peppers - washed, seeded and cut into strips
1/2 cup Burgundy cooking wine
2 tablespoons fresh chopped parsley
1 tablespoon each basil, oregano, thyme and pepper
1 large can crushed Italian tomatoes - do NOT drain. Use the liquid.
1 (6 oz.) can tomato paste

Garnish: 1/2 cup fresh grated romano cheese

Ready? HIT IT!

Preheat oven to 400 degrees

Line a large roasting pan with aluminum foil. Line it twice. (Why should you have to clean anything up? You've already done all the work!) Place all the chicken in the pan. Pour everything over the chicken. Spread all the ingredients evenly around. Bake, uncovered, for 30 minutes.

Remove from oven and baste. Spread vegetables around in the sauce, making sure that nothing is getting too brown. If vegetables are getting burnt, slide them under the chicken. Bake for another 20-30 minutes. Cover and allow to cool for 10 minutes before serving. Baste before you serve it. It makes the chicken and vegetables shine.

Remove to a big poultry platter. Sprinkle with cheese and garnish with fresh parsley sprigs. It looks like a buffet and tastes like a feast fit for a king or queen. Again - simple, low in fat, and magnificently flavorful!

Now... lie down and get ready. This is your "shining" moment!

TROUSER TROUT

Serves 4-6

This is a Mexican flavored fish dish and is **M-M-M-M good!** You can substitute halibut, flounder, cod, perch, or any fillet you want. It's a different way to serve fish.

6 fish fillets, washed. Pat dry with paper towels.
1/2 cup seasoned flour, (1 teaspoon each garlic powder, onion powder and pepper
    combined)
1/4 cup olive oil
2 cloves garlic, minced
1 large onion, chopped
1 small can green chilies
3 Italian plum tomatoes, washed and chopped
1 small green pepper, washed, seeded and chopped fine
1/2 teaspoon cumin seed
1 teaspoon black pepper
1/2 teaspoon oregano
2 tablespoons wine vinegar

Garnish: parsley sprigs, lemon wedges, cherry tomatoes

Optional: 3 tablespoons of oil for browning the fish in the frying pan. I do this for this recipe because I like a pan fried flavor for trout, but you can bake it without previously frying it.

Note: If a little more liquid is needed for this recipe, add some water and white wine.

Preheat oven to 350 degrees

Coat the fish fillets on both sides in seasoned flour. If pan frying, heat the oil in a large frying pan. Fry fish fillets for 2 minutes on each side. Remove to a baking dish that has been sprayed with non-stick cooking spray.

In the same frying pan, saute' all the other ingredients in 1/4 cup olive oil. Cook about 5-7 minutes, stirring occasionally. Adjust seasonings. Pour over fish fillets. Bake 15-20 minutes at 350 degrees. Garnish with parsley, lemon wedges and cherry tomatoes.

Remember, use any fish you want. Bake 10 minutes longer if you do not pan fry and also if the fish is a thick steak, like halibut or salmon. (I like a thinner fillet for this). This is a colorful and tasty recipe.

SUGGESTION: This sauce can be used over chicken. It is mild, but has a flavor that is delicious. I also serve it over cauliflower, spinach noodles, and salmon burgers.

Suggested Meal: Jizz Wizz
                        Greek Salad From Behind
                        Trouser Trout
                        Muffaletta
                        Whipped Cream with Utter Delight

LAY SAGNA

Serves 8

There are two dishes I especially like to make: Meatloaf and Lasagna. They are both economical, can be made ahead of time, can be used for leftovers, can feed 2-20 people, AND can be frozen and stored for a long time!! **As far as I am concerned, if you don't like them, I think therapy is in order for you, rather than food!!**

Below are several versions of Lay Sagna, but there are three basic parts you must have: noodles, cheese filling and sauce. What you do with your imagination is **ONLY TO YOUR CREDIT!**

1. <u>Noodle Part:</u>

This recipe is served in a 13 x 9 inch baking dish, but a 16 ounce box of lasagna noodles makes 2 casseroles, so prepare TWO of them! Boil the noodles (spinach, whole wheat, or regular) according to package directions, but add 1 tablespoon of olive oil to the water After noodles are cooked, drain, and <u>let soak in some cold water until ready to use.</u> They get real sticky and hard to separate if they get dry.

2. <u>Basic cheese filling:</u> (makes one casserole)

1 (1 lb.) container part-skim ricotta cheese
1 tablespoon olive oil
1/2 cup chopped onion
4 cloves garlic, minced
2 tablespoons fresh chopped parsley
1 tablespoon black pepper
6 ozs. (2 ozs. each) grated Swiss, mozzarella, <u>AND</u> romano cheeses.

Note: I grate all my cheeses. I use much less that way and they go a lot further. I also use a combination of cheeses to add a unique flavor, color, and texture.

Preheat oven to 350 degrees

In a medium frying pan, saute' the onion and garlic in 1 tablespoon olive oil for 3-5 minutes. Stir occasionally. In a large bowl, combine the onion and garlic mixture with ricotta, parsley and pepper. Reserve grated cheeses.

Note: If using my Marquis De Sade's Marinara Sauce, make it with 1 pound of ground beef or turkey. It is my favorite sauce for my meat version of Lay Sagna. Note: Use any tomato sauce you like, but add a can of mushrooms, extra garlic, and chopped tomatoes to give it a little more body. Again, Mrs. Boner just wants you to "play" with food. This is so simple you will make up a few casseroles and keep them on hand. Learn to cook in bulk. Make up several containers of the sauce and keep it too. Then you do not have to make sauce every time you need it!

continued on next page...

BASIC MEAT LAY SAGNA:

In a 13 x 9 inch baking dish, pour 1/2 cup sauce on the bottom. Layer with cooked noodles. Spread 1/3 of cheese mixture evenly over noodles and sprinkle with 1/3 of the grated cheeses. Pour sauce over cheese. Layer noodles, cheese and sauce. Repeat layering for about three layers. Top layer should have extra grated cheese on it.

Bake, uncovered, 40 minutes at 350 degrees until bubbly and golden brown. Let stand for 5-10 minutes in order to cool before serving.

Note: If you cover the casserole, it can stay for hours. Then reheat in microwave for a few minutes. If frozen, bring to room temperature and then microwave or bake for 20 minutes at 350 degrees, covered.

VEGETARIAN VERSION: (Add to Ricotta cheese mixture)
Use basic tomato sauce recipe. Just omit meat.

1/4 cup olive oil and some water, if needed
1/2 cup chopped onion
3 cloves garlic, minced
1/2 cup chopped fresh tomatoes
1/2 cup sliced mushrooms, fresh
1/2 cup chopped parsley; or 1 cup chopped spinach; or 1 cup chopped green peppers; or 1 cup chopped broccoli

In a large frying pan, saute' all the ingredients. Cook and stir about 5 minutes. Add a little extra oregano, basil, thyme and crushed red pepper. Add this mixture to the ricotta filling.

Prepare frozen vegetables as package directs and saute'.

Layer according to directions...noodles, cheese, sauce, etc. End with a layer of noodles and sauce. Top with grated cheese.

What a colorful and delicious dish! All you did was add some vegetables to create a completely different-looking casserole!

SUGGESTION: You can add 1 cup of cooked shrimp, cooked chicken strips, tuna or salmon for even more variety. I have used every possible combination of ingredients in this dish. But the basics are: noodles, cheese filling and sauce.

Wait until you taste the tuna and shrimp combination with garlic and onion in the ricotta layer! And, oh what color you have with the broccoli, spinach, parsley, zucchini, and mushrooms, which you will saute' in a garlic/olive oil blend.

Suggested Meal: Cuntaloupe with Assorted Meats
                         Cock Rings
                         Lay Sagna
                         Spermoni

MAMMARY MOUNDS

Serves 4

These are **BIG!!** Stuffed, and full-bodied: More than a handful, and not to mention, I ate the "hole" thing! It's stuffed eggplant made with ground turkey and rice! A real man's dish!

2 medium eggplants, 1/2 per serving - leave the skin on
1 pound ground turkey, veal or sirloin
2 tablespoons olive oil , (1 tablespoon for browning the turkey; 1 tablespoon for cooking the vegetables)
1 cup cooked brown rice or white rice, prepared as package directs
2-4 cloves garlic, minced
1 large onion, finely chopped
1 tablespoon pepper
1 teaspoon crushed red pepper
2 Italian plum tomatoes, washed and chopped
1 tablespoon chopped parsley

Topping: Tomato sauce, parsley, grated romano cheese

With a large sharp knife, remove tops and cut each eggplant in half. Carefully spoon out the eggplant to within 1/2 inch of the skin. Sprinkle salt lightly into eggplant shells and leave for 1/2 hour to bleed and remove all bitterness. Press paper towels over eggplant to completely absorb moisture. Chop eggplant pulp and combine with onion and garlic in a large bowl. Brown turkey or other meat in 1 tablespoon olive oil. Drain off fat.

Note: The most important thing to remember about eggplant is that they can be bitter. Salt does help this problem, so whenever you prepare eggplant, sprinkle with salt, wait 30 minutes and blot with paper towels.

Preheat oven to 350 degrees

In a large frying pan, saute' onion, garlic and eggplant in 1 tablespoon of olive oil for several minutes. Add turkey, pepper, tomatoes, and parsley, and continue cooking until onions are golden brown. Remove and combine with rice. Mix thoroughly. Adjust seasonings to taste. Place eggplant halves in a large casserole or roasting pan. Add 1/2 inch water. Spoon eggplant mixture into halves, forming a mound.

Cover and bake in the oven for 30 minutes. Remove cover and continue baking for 30 minutes longer or until eggplant is tender. Depending on the size of the eggplant, the cooking time may vary 10-20 minutes, more or less.

continued on next page...

When cooked, place on a serving platter and spoon heated sauce over the top. Sprinkle with cheese and garnish with parsley.

Note: The water in the pan is optional. Sometimes I use a little olive oil to prevent sticking. **Make sure the eggplants are packed tightly and fully stuffed. Also make sure that they don't fall over.**

SUGGESTION: I like to use ground veal and turkey. I also have used pasta instead of rice. Mixed vegetables can be substituted and bread crumbs incorporated to keep the mixture together.

<u>Suggested Meal:</u>   Cuntaloupe With Assorted Meats
                                Seize Me Salad
                                Garlic Bread
                                Mammary Mounds
                                Spermoni

BEEF STROKE ME OFF

Serves 4-6

This is my version of the "classic dish", Beef Stroganoff. Mine has been "stroked off"! All the ingredients are mixed together and placed in a casserole dish. It's easy and ready to go when you are. I am a big casserole eater because I like to get my protein and carbohydrates together and not have too much clean up. Get off on this tasty casserole!

Ingredients:

1 (8 ounce) package of egg noodles - prepare as package directs. Spinach noodles or artichoke pasta may also be used, but green noodles may look like you "puked" in this dish!

1-1/2 pounds ground turkey or good ground sirloin
1 tablespoon vegetable oil
1 large onion, chopped
2-4 cloves garlic, minced
1 medium green pepper, washed, seeded and finely chopped
8 ounces tomato sauce, no-salt variety
1/2 cup fresh mushroom slices
1 teaspoon black pepper
1 teaspoon paprika
1 cup (1% milkfat) cottage cheese
1/2 cup lite sour cream or yogurt

Topping:

1/4 cup chopped green onions (scallions)
1/2 cup shredded Swiss cheese, low-fat, reduced-calorie

Preheat oven to 350 degrees

Prepare egg noodles as package directs. Sprinkle with garlic powder, if desired. Saute' the meat in a large frying pan, in 1 tablespoon of vegetable oil. Add mushrooms, onions, garlic, and green peppers. Cook about 5-7 minutes until vegetables are done. Stir occasionally. Drain off liquid. In a large bowl, combine meat/vegetable mixture with tomato sauce and seasonings.

Spray a large casserole dish with non-stick cooking spray. In another bowl, mix noodles, cottage cheese, and sour cream. Layer as follows: Noodles, meat, noodles, and then top with the rest of the meat. Sprinkle with additional cheese and chopped scallions. If you do not want to layer this casserole, you can stir it all together. It's G-R-E-A-T either way!!

Bake, uncovered, in a 350 degree oven for 30-45 minutes until bubbly. Cover with foil and let cool for 10 minutes. "By getting your beef stroked before dinner, you can get the main event off sooner!!

Note: I like this casserole reheated in the microwave the next day. It is a great dish for company. You can make it up for fifty at a time!

BUFF WELLINGTON

Serves 4 as a main dish
(8 as an appetizer or side dish)

My "Buff" is not like any Buff Wellington you have had before. Most buffs have a pastry envelope surrounding the meat. In this recipe, my meat surrounds a wonderful filling, so My Buff is meat and My Wellington is soft, tasty, and worth waiting for....Rolled up slices of turkey and a stuffing of oranges, broccoli, and rice. **No better Buff in town!**

Ingredients for Filling:

8 slices of turkey breast, sliced thick enough to roll securely
1 cup chopped broccoli. Steam frozen, chopped broccoli as package directs before
          using.
1 (11 oz.) can mandarin orange sections, drained. Reserve liquid.
1/2 cup low-calorie sweet and sour dressing, French dressing, or Catalina dressing
1 teaspoon ground ginger
2 tablespoons chopped parsley
2 tablespoons chopped green onions
1/4 cup raisins
1 cup cooked white or brown rice

Combine for Sauce:

1/4 cup mandarin orange juice
1/2 cup orange marmalade, low-sugar variety
Juice of 1 lemon

Garnish: Orange slices, parsley sprigs

Preheat oven to 350 degrees. Spray an 11 x 9 inch baking dish with non-stick cooking spray; a 9 inch round pan is OK to use as well.

In a large bowl, combine broccoli, mandarin oranges, dressing, parsley, onions, ginger, raisins and rice. Place 1/4 cup of the mixture on a slice of turkey. Roll up. Place seam side down in dish. Secure with a plain toothpick. Pour on the sauce. Bake, uncovered, for 15 minutes, remove from oven and baste. Bake 10-15 minutes longer.

Place a slice of fresh orange and parsley sprig on each roll. **Aah!** Low-calorie, gorgeous, and as pretty a buff as you will ever see!

SUGGESTION: You may have extra stuffing left over. Stuff a tomato or green pepper with it! This is a good luncheon dish, so one roll may be enough. If using for dinner, 2 rolls are adequate. It can also be an appetizer by cutting each roll in 2 parts. You would then have 16 rolls. (Smart!) You can substitute lots of other ingredients into the rice. Play with a recipe like this.

Suggested Meal: Hot Lips/Hot Hips
                                   Shake It Baby Salad
                                   Buff Wellington
                                   Knight Stick

M-19

MANICOCKME
OR
MACHO MANICOTTI

Serves 6-8

This makes 12 shells (2 per person). My friends are real piggies, so they eat for two. They need three shells each! If you buy prepared shells, they are great as well.

Note: Recipe for Marquis De Sade's Marinara Sauce in chapter on "Salad Dressings and Sauces". Or, use any good tomato sauce.

Shell Recipe:

3 eggs at room temperature
3/4 cup unsifted flour
3/4 cup water

Note: I do not like using egg yolks and white flour, but these are very tasty shells. If you have the time to make your own, they are so good.

In a medium bowl, combine the ingredients. Beat with electric mixer until smooth. Let stand 1/2 hour. Heat in a non-stick 8-9 inch frying pan. The pan should be very hot before adding batter. Pour 3 tablespoons of the batter into the hot skillet. Quickly rotate the pan to evenly distribute batter. When bubbles appear on the top of the pancake and the sides peel away, remove pancake to waxed paper and cool. It takes 45 seconds to 1 minute to make the shells. A hot skillet is necessary. They get done quickly and come out of the pan easily.

Note: If using prepared shells, cook according to package directions.

Filling:

1 (1 lb.) container part-skim, low-fat ricotta cheese, or half ricotta and half (1% milkfat) cottage cheese (8 ounces each)
1 (6-8 oz.) package part-skim mozzarella cheese - grated; or cut into small pieces
1/3 cup parmesan cheese
2 egg whites, or one egg
1 tablespoon minced garlic; or 1 tablespoon garlic powder
2 tablespoons chopped parsley, fresh
Black pepper to taste
1/4 cup grated parmesan cheese - for topping

Preheat oven to 350 degrees

Spread 1/2 cup tomato sauce on bottom of a 13 x 9 inch casserole dish. Combine all the filling ingredients in a large bowl except the 1/4 cup parmesan cheese. Blend well. Add about 1/4 cup filling to center of each shell. Roll up carefully, secure seam and try not to let any filling drip out of the sides.

continued on next page...

Place shells seam side down in dish. Pour 2-3 cups of sauce over shells. Sprinkle with extra parmesan cheese and bake, uncovered, for 30 minutes until bubbly and well done. Wait about 5 minutes to serve; it tastes so good when it is a little cooler.

Note: I like garlic, so I always serve my Italian dishes with a side of chopped garlic. When you sprinkle it on cooling pasta, you get a rush that only gourmet cooks can appreciate. Do not make any excuses for your breath! After you have served this dish and you tell them that you made the shells, the filling, and the sauce from scratch, and it took you no time at all (do not tell them you made this recipe a month before and froze it), they will probably take you to the nearest department store and buy you a trinket! **In fact, this is so easy to make that you should make several casseroles and get a LOT of trinkets!**

SUGGESTION: Want to hear a real tickler? Add 2 cans of water- packed tuna (drain thoroughly) to the filling mixture and make TUNA MANICOCKME. Do not change anything else. Just add tuna and proceed as for regular recipe.

<u>Suggested Meal:</u>   Eatin' at the Y Spread
Hot-Flashin' Antipasto
Manicockme
Cunt Candy and Throw Me Down and Fuck Me Fudge

QUICHE ME LORRAINE

Serves 4

This one is definitely different. Not your traditional quiche. Great for lunch or appetizers. Whoever Lorraine is, she is <u>One Lucky Lady!</u>

2 cups zucchini, sliced very thin. 1 cup of yellow squash and one cup of green zucchini look very pretty in this recipe.
1 cup (1% milk fat) cottage cheese
1 egg plus 2 egg whites
1/2 cup skim milk
1/2 teaspoon pepper
2 cloves garlic, minced
2 cups cooked rice - white, brown or wild
3 ounces part-skim mozzarella cheese, grated
1 cup Marquis De Sade's Marinara Sauce (see index) or tomato sauce of your choice.

Preheat oven to 350 degrees

In your food processor, slice zucchini or squash. In a large sauce pan and in boiling water, steam vegetables for 5 minutes using a steamer basket. Drain very thoroughly. <u>Remove excess water</u>. In food processor, combine cottage cheese and eggs until smooth. Add garlic, pepper, milk and squash. Blend thoroughly.

Spray a round 10 inch baking dish with non-stick cooking spray. Press rice on bottom of plate. Pour squash mixture over the rice. Sprinkle with cheese. Bake 350 degrees for 45 minutes until set. Cool. Wait several minutes before cutting. Serve with tomato sauce.

SUGGESTION: Use ricotta cheese instead of cottage cheese, low-fat Swiss cheese instead of mozzarella. (I like to use both cheeses - Swiss AND Mozzarella in this recipe) Scallions also look good and add an onion flavor.

<u>Suggested Meal:</u>   Nipple Nuggets
                Seize Me Salad
                Quiche Me Lorraine
                Chocolate Orgasm

FONDLED BREAST OF CHICKEN

Serves 4 - double recipe for 8

Ecstasy!! Heaven!! Health food should <u>NOT</u> be boring. I could eat this dish cold, dry, drunk, horny, starved for sex, PMS... <u>ANYWAY YOU CAN GIVE IT TO ME!</u>

The coating on these breasts will seal the juices in, so take the fat off for this chicken recipe.

4 large chicken breasts - real chicken breasts, not the "phony" ones.

<u>Marinate in the following:</u>

1/2 cup frozen concentrated orange juice
1 egg, slightly beaten
1 teaspoon garlic powder

<u>Coating:</u>

2 cups crushed corn flake crumbs
1/2 cup shredded coconut
2 tablespoons light brown sugar, 25% reduced-calorie
1 tablespoon curry powder (you may want to use less)
1 tablespoon fresh chopped garlic
2 tablespoons melted butter, margarine or oil (this to be added to marinade later)

Garnish: Orange slices, parsley sprigs, raisins

In a large baking dish, marinate the chicken several hours, turning occasionally. Keep refrigerated. Remove the chicken from the liquid. Reserve liquid. If you skinned the chicken - good for you! If you didn't, you'll have to work it off later!

Preheat oven to 350 degrees

Mix all the coating ingredients together. Press the mixture into chicken. Adjust any seasonings. Place back in baking or casserole dish. Mix melted butter with reserved marinade and drizzle over the chicken. Bake, covered, for 30 minutes. Remove from oven. Uncover and baste. Return to oven and bake 20-30 minutes longer, uncovered, until chicken is done. The cooking time may vary for this recipe, depending upon the size of the "tittys". 45 minutes to one hour is about right. <u>Eyeball it!</u> The coating will keep the breasts moist. (Mrs. Boner hates dry breasts!) Serve on a large platter with orange slices, parsley sprigs and raisins.

Note: Use an entire chicken, halves, or any other parts you may want for this recipe. The coating is delicious. In fact, you can use this recipe for fish fillets.

Want to get intense? Use this recipe on DUCK. Coconut Duck Parts... **ORGASMIC!**

<u>Suggested Meal:</u>   Fondled Breast of Chicken
Polynesian Pea Pea Pods
Down and Dirty Rice
"Exhaustion" (to be announced in second book!)

"CUM" CAKES

Serves 4-6

No, it's not what you think! They are salmon burgers. Ha! Ha! Gotcha on this one! These are so easy and nutritious. They will be glad they did come (your guests, of course!) for lunch.

1 (15-1/2 oz.) can salmon, drained, de-boned and flaked. Reserve liquid. Some people like their burgers more moist than others.
1 cup Matzo meal, or 1 cup 40 calorie light bread crumbs
2 egg whites (substituted for 1 egg)
1/4 cup chopped scallions
1 clove garlic, minced
Juice of 1/2 lemon or 1 tablespoon lemon juice
Pepper, parsley to taste

Note: If you dare to be different use a few drops of hot pepper seasoning. I sometimes use a little olive oil and butter to saute' these burgers in, but non-stick cooking spray works fine as well.

In a large bowl, mix all the ingredients together. Shape into 6 or 8 patties. In a large frying pan, if using oil, heat. If using spray, spray before heating the pan. Fry about 4-5 minutes on each side. Remove to a pretty platter.

Garnish with lemon wedges, parsley sprigs and/or deviled eggs.

Serve on whole wheat rolls with "Cocktail Sauce" (see index) tomato slices, shredded lettuce, raw onion, pickles and horseradish.

Note: Burgers are burgers. Everyone likes them. Salmon is flavorful and so easy to use. Salmon burgers are a great main dish. Serve them with tomato sauce on Angel Hair Pasta. **Elegant AND easy!**

SUBSTITUTIONS: (For Salmon)

1 (15-1/2 oz.) can water-packed tuna, drained and washed in a colander to remove excess sodium.

1 (15-1/2 oz.) can Jack Mackerel. It is less expensive than salmon. Add extra fresh lemon juice to the mixture and it is delicious. Nobody would know! So what if they did know! Salmon is VERY expensive. You are practical, smart AND creative!

SUBSTITUTIONS: (For Rolls)

Bagels, pita pockets, rice cakes

Suggested Meal: (How about a Buffet of fish smells.....)

                         Lip Drip Dip
                         "Cum" Cakes
                         Tongued Tuna
                         Eat My Cherry, Please!

SENSUOUS SNAPPER

Serves 4

"I hate fish! I hate the look! I hate the smell! I hate the feel! I hate the hate!"
BUT... this recipe actually sounds delicious - and it is! I had to put 2 fish recipes in this book (one male and one female. You figure it out - which one is which: Trouser Trout or Sensuous Snapper!)

People in the health awareness field and nutrition business will try to get you to eat fish a lot more. **Well, not me!** But... for those snappy people, here is your sensuous fish dish.

2 pounds snapper fillets
Flour
Black pepper
1/4 cup olive oil
Juice of one fresh lemon
1/4 cup white wine
1 tablespoon chopped fresh parsley
1 tablespoon rosemary
1 tablespoon oregano
3 medium white onions, sliced thin
4 cloves garlic, minced
1/4 cup parmesan cheese

Garnish: lemon wedges, tomato sauce, and extra cheese

Preheat oven to 350 degrees

Spray your baking dish with non-stick cooking spray. The size of the baking dish depends on the size of the fillets. Shake fillets in flour and season with pepper. Place in the baking dish. Saute' onion and garlic in olive oil. Add all the other ingredients, except cheese. When onions are golden brown, pour over fish. Sprinkle with grated parmesan cheese and extra black pepper. Bake for 20-25 minutes, uncovered.

Garnish with lemon wedges, tomato sauce, and extra cheese.

SUBSTITUTIONS FOR SNAPPER: Whitefish, sole fillets, grouper, flounder, and/or chicken breasts.

SUGGESTION: You can also add several chopped Italian plum tomatoes, mushroom slices, or saute' green pepper slices with the onions. Use red wine in the recipe instead of white. It's a versatile and flavorful fish dish!

Suggested Meal: 69 Spread
                         Flagellow
                         Sensuous Snapper
                         Deep Throat Apple Pie

MOUNT-ME MEATLOAF

Serves 6-8

Meatloaves are fun. There is no rule to follow except to have it be moist and firm... **like a good woman!** The size of the baking pan can vary - whatever you like... **kind of like a good man!** Mount-Me Meatloaf is healthy, flavorful, very easy to make, and a nice change. Keep it low-fat.

2 lbs. ground turkey
2 egg whites. This substitutes for one egg, as I do not use yolks unless I have to.
3/4 cup dry oatmeal - plain variety
1 medium onion, chopped fine
2-4 cloves of garlic, minced
Pepper, parsley, or any salt-free seasoning to taste
1 (10 oz.) package of frozen chopped spinach (squeeze out all excess water)
1 (4 oz.) can of no-salt tomato sauce

Note: Add extra water if the consistency of the meatloaf mixture is too dry.

Preheat oven to 375 degrees

In a large bowl, mix all ingredients together. Spray casserole dish with non-stick cooking spray. Press into prepared dish. Bake for 45 minutes to one hour. The baking time may vary, depending upon the size of the dish. Let stand 5 minutes before cutting.

SUGGESTION: This recipe makes 2 smaller meatloaves. Keep an extra one for leftovers, another dinner, or to freeze. Always make more than you need. You will save time later. I like to make this one in a 13 x 9 inch baking dish, as it serves 6-8 nicely.

SUBSTITUTIONS:

For Turkey: Ground veal, pork, sirloin or any combination of each.

For Oatmeal: 1 cup whole wheat matzo crumbs. Make them in the food processor
                 from sheets of whole wheat matzo.
                 2 slices of day old 40 calorie light bread made into crumbs
                 2/3 cup wheat bran or wheat germ
                 3/4 cup bran cereal
                 1 cup cooked rice or cooked pasta

For Spinach: 1 (15 oz.) can red kidney beans - drained
                 1 cup grated carrot
                 1 package of frozen mixed vegetables

continued on next page...

SUGGESTED SAUCES ON THE SIDE:

Barbecue sauce
Low-salt tomato sauce
Non-fat plain yogurt mixed with horseradish
Mustard and horseradish

Note: I try to keep my additional condiments and sauces low-fat. Ketchup is not "fat" fattening, but does have a high sugar content. Mustard, horseradish, and barbecue sauce have a moderate sodium content but are basically non-fat. Watch what you put on your food. Extras have a lot of calories. Some are empty calories, and many do contain sugar. __*Just think before you reach for it!*__ *(A personal comment from Mrs. Boner!)*

Suggested Meal: The Six Incher
                     Chew Me
                     Mount-Me Meatloaf
                     Schmucks
                     Golden Ram

Vegetables, Beans, Rice, Pasta
(Stop I can't take anymore!)

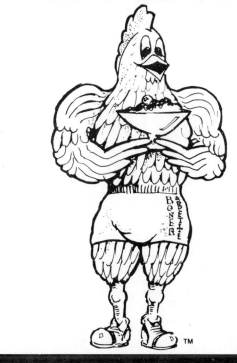

PUSSY POTATOES/STUFF 'EM TWICE - EAT 'EM ONCE

Serves 4

These are for the real connoisseurs of eating...moist AND flavorful. Do them ahead and reheat. GO DOWN ON THEM and you will never eat a plain potato again! This recipe is for white baking potatoes. You'll have to wait for the sweet potato recipe! (It will be in the next book). However, **it will be a pussy potato worth waiting for!!**

Note: **Do not microwave these potatoes.**

Double Stuffed Baked Potatoes

4 large baking potatoes - washed, scrubbed and dried. Prick twice with fork.

1/2 cup (1% milk fat) cottage cheese. Ricotta may also be used.
1/4 cup non-fat plain yogurt
2 tablespoons fresh chopped parsley
1/4 cup chopped scallions - green onions
1 tablespoon black pepper
1 tablespoon butter substitute (dry)
1 teaspoon each garlic powder, onion powder, dry mustard
1/4-1/3 cup shredded Lorraine Swiss cheese
Paprika

Preheat oven to 425 degrees

Bake potatoes for one hour in a 425 degree oven. Let cool for one hour. In your food processor, whip all the other ingredients, except Swiss and paprika. Slit potato along top and keeping 1/2 inch of the shell, gently scoop out the inside of the potato. Whip potato mixture with other ingredients for a minute. Stuff potatoes with this mixture. Top with Swiss cheese and paprika. You choose the amount of the cheese. When reheating, bake at 400 degrees for 15 minutes until potato is heated through; when the cheese has melted and the top is golden brown, it's done and ready to eat!

SUGGESTION: I add a can of small shrimp to this mixture and it is great. You can also add a can of mushroom slices or spinach. But the basic stuffing mixture is a lot less caloric than sour cream and butter.

JAMMED YAMS

Serves 8

A HOLEY DAY FAVORITE

This recipe is named because I jam a lot of ingredients into a casserole dish and bake. Use sweet potatoes or yams. This recipe is not only delicious, but rich in vitamin A, vitamin C, potassium, and is high in fiber. These potatoes have been linked in the prevention of diseases, from "lack of hard-on" to "too much hard-on" and "way too much hard-in"!

You can beat them, mash them, cube them, ball them, (I like THIS one) bake them, or eat them cold - as I do - in sandwiches. **They are great!** My husband can't eat a lot of them because he says they are TOO rich, but he says the same thing about me!! However, when he DOES eat, he eats well! (An inside joke!)

Scrub and peel 4 large sweet potatoes or yams. Cut into large cubes or 1/2 inch slices. You may par-boil potatoes for 15 minutes. Cool and then cut.

1 (16 oz.) package of frozen carrots or 6-8 medium carrots, peeled and cut diagonally
    into 1 inch pieces
1 medium onion, chopped finely
2-4 cloves garlic, minced
2 Granny Smith apples - cored, pared and cut into cubes. Dip them in lemon juice to
    prevent premature darkening (sound sexy?)
1/2 cup applesauce
1/2 cup orange juice (you may use concentrate, just dilute beforehand)
1 tablespoon butter or peanut oil
1 tablespoon honey
1 tablespoon light brown sugar - 25% reduced-calorie variety
1/2 cup raisins, dates or prunes (pitted) - we don't want any broken teeth!

Mix together the following: cinnamon, nutmeg, ginger, orange peel. Amounts vary, depending upon individual taste.

Preheat oven to 400 degrees

Spray a 13 x 9 inch baking dish with non-stick cooking spray. Except for raisins, toss all ingredients, including spices, together in a large bowl. Place mixture in prepared baking dish. Bake in a 400 degree oven for 30 minutes, covered. Remove from oven. Baste, and add raisins. Add more water if necessary.

Return to oven and bake uncovered for an additional 30 minutes. You can cover this recipe and bake for the entire hour to keep the raisins from getting burnt. Oven temperatures vary and the size of the dish can change the baking time. Test for doneness with fork. Let cool. I baste every 15 minutes, so I don't cover mine at all. If potatoes are par-boiled, the cooking time will take about 45 minutes instead of 1 hour. Baste after 20 minutes of cooking and bake an additional 25 minutes uncovered.

*Note: This recipe is excellent the next day. Reheat in the microwave a few minutes. It tastes even BETTER... all the ingredients have been blended together....***Y-U-M!!!!**

FRENCHED FRIES

Serves 4 (generously)

I have always felt that if you were going to eat a calorie, make it a good one! French fries are no exception. If you eat them, they should be "sinfully" rich and LOADED with ketchup and salt. Go all the way or do not go at all!

2 large baking potatoes or sweet potatoes
Any good oil, vegetable cooking oil or non-stick, non-fat cooking spray
Pepper, garlic and onion powders, paprika, salt-free seasonings, popcorn seasonings, or chili powder

Note: I keep my olive oil in the refrigerator to prevent it from getting an odor. It gets cloudy and hard, but when brought to room temperature it is fresh and natural.
I have found an interesting way to use less oil and still have quality and great flavor. Get a sprayer bottle and fill it with your favorite oil. Crush garlic cloves in it, and you now have an easy and economical way to spray a good oil on your salads or in your pans, to give it EXTRA zest! I have several spray bottles labeled with my different oils and vinegars. It's practical, easy and convenient. I highly recommend the idea!

Preheat oven to 375 degrees

I will use the safflower oil from my spray bottle. Spray a large baking sheet lightly with oil. Spread oil around. Peel potatoes and cut into 1/4 to 1/2 inch strips, depending upon whether you like them thick or thin. Spread them evenly on the baking pan. Lightly spray them with oil. Season with any of your favorite condiments. Bake in a 375 degree oven for 20 minutes. Turn carefully and continue baking 20 minutes more. You may also put them under the broiler for a few minutes to get them darker. These will not be very crispy, but they WILL be tasty and non-greasy. You CAN have some fat in your diet, especially when it is "quality fat".

Remove fries from oven and add a little extra garlic or onion powder. Serve in a basket with a large napkin under them. They look so pretty!

SUGGESTION: If you want to use your food processor, you can slice the potatoes in it and make them like home fries. Toss them in the oil and seasonings the same way, and then bake for 15 minutes. Turn them. Bake an additional 15 minutes. Remember, these are thinner and will take less cooking time. They are now called, "American/ Frenched Fries".

FRIED TATTAS

Serves 6-8

I had a friend once who liked to call women's tits, "tattas". You can name them, number them, etc., but in the end, they still are "fried bean cakes"! Tits or Tattas... they are great in your hands AND in your mouths!

3 cups canned red kidney or pinto beans, drained and mashed
3 cloves garlic, minced
1 large onion, chopped finely
1/2 green pepper, chopped finely
1 teaspoon tabasco or - for the adventurous - my favorite: 1 pickled jalapeno pepper, rinsed, seeded and chopped
2 tablespoons vegetable oil, butter, margarine or non-stick cooking spray
1/4 cup shredded Colby cheese

In food processor or blender, add all the ingredients, except oil and cheese. Process until well blended. If you want to make these patties a little firmer for more shape, you can add a little whole wheat flour or bread crumbs, but not too much.

Heat oil or melt butter in a large frying pan over medium-high heat. I use non-stick spray and the patties come out just as good. Form bean mixture into 6-8 large patties, or as many small ones as you can make. Fry several minutes on each side until browned. (Be careful turning them). Add a little more oil if necessary or more spray.

Serve with a sprinkle of cheese and a little extra garlic powder. A side of salsa is also great, or a bit of yogurt.

SUGGESTION: This is a simple side dish or appetizer. If you do not want to make this recipe into patties, press the mixture into the frying pan and keep stirring until heated through. Then it's a GREAT bean dip... and from a pan!

FRIED BEAN PATTIES OR REFRIED BEAN DIP... TWO FOR THE PRICE OF ONE!

Note: Use Fried Tattas on Whoretilla Chips and on Nasty Nachos with Holey Guacamole and Pumpin' Picante (see index).

POOPY PINTOS

Serves 8-10

<u>The poopy comes from the jalapenos. The more peppers, the more poopy!!</u>

1 lb. of pinto beans - any kind or a combination of white and pink. About 2-1/2 cups dry.
6 cups of water
3-6 cloves garlic, minced
1 large onion, chopped
2 pickled jalapenos - seeded, rinsed thoroughly, and finely chopped
1 (8 oz.) can tomatoes, cut into large pieces
1 tablespoon chopped parsley

In a large kettle or Dutch oven, soak beans overnight in the water. Do not drain. Add all the other ingredients. Bring to a full boil and let simmer for 1-1/2 to 2 hours.

This is a great recipe made ahead of time! It freezes well and can be used for so many purposes. It is high in complex carbohydrates and low in fat. Eat it at night and get relief in the morning.! **Better than a prune cocktail!**

Note: Beans are great for you. If you keep them simple and do them from scratch, they are easy and delicious. Beans and rice are a perfect protein. The energy that you get from eating beans will keep you pumpin' long into the night!!

SUGGESTION: You can whip your "Poopy Pintos" in the food processor after the beans have cooled. You may have to drain them before you process. This is ANOTHER version of a bean dip that can be used a different way. Spread this dip on cucumber and tomato slices, on bagel chips or melba crackers. <u>Start out with hot beans as a vegetable and end up with a dip the next day. OLE'! (Oh! I-a-y!)</u>

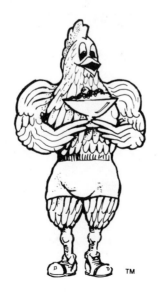

TM

DOWN AND DIRTY RICE

Serves 6-8

If you have never cooked with brown rice, it is quite different. You'll find the rice firmer and harder than white rice. I only use brown rice because I like it firm and hard... just ask my husband!! BUT - if you want to use white rice, just cook according to package directions. I also cook my rice in low-sodium bouillon (10 mg. sodium per package.) Use chicken or beef.

To cook brown rice: For 1 cup uncooked rice use 2-1/2 cups of water. This may vary, depending on what other ingredients you add and whether you like your rice moist or dry.

Ingredients:

1 cup uncooked brown rice
2 (packages) low-sodium bouillon, mixed with 2-1/2 cups of water
2 scallions, chopped finely
2 cloves garlic, minced
1 tablespoon fresh parsley, chopped
1 (4 oz.) can mushrooms, rinsed thoroughly
Pepper, rosemary, thyme, etc. Add your own herbs when you add the rice.

In a large pot or Dutch oven, bring water to a full boil. Add the rice and all the other ingredients. Cover and bring back to a full boil. Reduce heat and simmer about 45 minutes to 1 hour. I like my rice moist.

Note: Low-sodium bouillon cubes and packages can be obtained in either the soup or diet section of your market.

SUGGESTION: I also like rice cold, so I make this dish up and chill it. Then I add a little sesame oil, chopped celery, scallions, and some sweet and sour sauce. It tastes fantastic with chicken or tuna, in a tomato or green pepper cup. Again, make a lot up. It keeps well, and you can do so much with this basic recipe!

HAIR PASTA WITH PESTO SAUCE

Serves 4

Everyone is on the pesto bandwagon! Angel hair pasta looks... Oh! So elegant! Oh! So delightfully feminine! So, our Pesto is on our Hair Pasta.

Angel Hair Pasta takes only a few minutes to make. Therefore, make the sauce up first.

Note: Pesto Sauce comes ready made and some are quite good. I like to make my own sauce because I add extra garlic. Also, I like the freshness when it is made from scratch.

1 (8 ounce) package of Angel Hair Pasta - 2 oz. (dry) per serving

Ingredients for Pesto Sauce:

1 cup firmly packed fresh snipped, chopped basil
1/2 cup fresh parsley, chopped
1/2 cup fresh parmesan cheese, grated finely
1/2 cup pine nuts, walnuts or almonds, chopped. I think there is no substitute for pine
    nuts.
3-4 cloves garlic, minced
1/2 cup olive oil

In your food processor, combine all the ingredients except oil. Turn on and off until a paste forms. Gradually add the oil until the paste is the consistency of soft butter. Keep the processor on while adding oil. Put in a tightly sealed container. Refrigerate until ready to use. Bring to room temperature one hour before using for my recipe.

Cook pasta as package directs. Drain, but reserve 1/4 cup cooking liquid. Add pesto sauce to pasta immediately. **Great!**

Serve with extra cheese and sprinkle with additional pine nuts.

Note: This recipe is beautiful, colorful AND delicious. The beauty of this sauce is that it can be spooned out and served on fish, chicken, salmon burgers, or even on broiled tomatoes. Warm it up and then spread it on toast or Italian bread. Olive oil gets very solid when cold. It does get soft again when brought to room temperature. It will stay fresher - longer - in the refrigerator.

Note: Make a large portion of pesto sauce and keep it in the refrigerator for many special dishes.

MOUNTAIN OYSTERS

Serves 8

I've never understood where this name comes from or why. If there were oysters in the mountains we wouldn't have to eat these slimy little bastards from our polluted waters! Well, these oysters are 100% healthy and you do not have to go deep sea diving to get them. They are stuffed whole onions.

Note: You can substitute any vegetable or pasta in this recipe. Whole onions are beautiful to serve and easy to go down.

Ingredients:

8 medium to large white onions
1 tablespoon butter and 1 low-salt bouillon cube, dissolved in 1/2 cup water
2-4 cloves garlic, minced
1 large green pepper, chopped finely
1 large red pepper, chopped finely
1 large zucchini, chopped finely
1/2 cup corn; or 1/2 cup peas
1/2 cup fresh bread crumbs or bread stuffing; or 1/2 cup brown or white rice
1 tablespoon black pepper
1 tablespoon parsley
1/2 teaspoon rosemary

Cut the tops off of the onions. Leave the bottoms on to keep the onion intact. Peel off the most outer layer of skin by making a vertical slit in skin and pulling it off. In a large Dutch oven, boil onions for 10 minutes. Carefully remove and let cool thoroughly. **Onions are hard to handle when hot...Just like a good woman!!**

In a large frying pan, saute' all vegetables in butter and bouillon water until vegetables are tender - usually about 5-8 minutes. In a large bowl, combine vegetables, bread crumbs, and/or rice and seasonings.

Preheat oven to 350 degrees

Gently remove the innermost core of the onion with a spoon. Leave about 4-5 layers of onion intact to make a good shell. Chop the removed onion and add to the other ingredients. Spoon mixture into onion shells. Pack it in, but be careful not to break open the onions. <u>You may have extra filling, so stuff it in something else or eat it cold!</u>

Spray your baking dish with non-stick cooking spray. Add about 1/4 inch of water to keep onions from drying out. Bake, uncovered in oven for 20-30 minutes. Use a dish that does not crowd the onions.

Note: It is better to use a larger baking dish so that the onions get cooked and the mixture gets hot. Oven temperatures vary, so keep an eye on them. It is still a foolproof vegetable and delicious. Sprinkle with chopped parsley, garlic or onion powder, or even shredded low-fat Swiss cheese.

COCK TEASERS

Serves 4

There is no teasing your guests when you serve the real thing... long... hard... AND stuffed. Ready to put in your mouth and eat ... ever so s-l-o-w-l-y because the flavor is so fine and the feeling so good!! Keep telling yourself this over and over again.

Ingredients:

2 good-sized zucchini - whatever looks good to you. (Enjoy THIS part of the recipe!)
1/2 cup chopped onion
3 cloves garlic, minced
1/4 cup mushroom slices - canned are OK for this, but I like fresh slices.
1/4 cup chopped red pepper
1/2 cup chopped yellow squash
1 tablespoon black pepper
1 tablespoon basil
2 tablespoons fresh parmesan cheese, grated (optional)

Garnish: cherry tomatoes and parsley sprigs

Preheat oven to 350 degrees

Cut zucchini in half. Scoop out the pulp, leaving the shell intact. You can use a melon "baller" or grapefruit spoon. If you want to wait until the zucchini are steamed, the pulp does come out easier. Add 1/2 inch of water to a large frying pan. Heat to boiling. Place zucchini halves in pan and steam cut side down 5-7 minutes until soft. Remove from pan.

When cool, scoop out pulp, if you didn't before. Either way you get the pulp out is fine, but be careful to leave a solid shell. Reserve the pulp.

Spray a large frying pan with non-stick cooking spray. Saute' zucchini pulp, all the other ingredients, and seasonings, except the cheese. Cook 3-5 minutes. If vegetable mixture is watery, drain or blot with paper towels. If you need more liquid, add water or white wine.

Spoon back into shells and sprinkle with cheese. Bake, uncovered, in a 350 degree oven for 15-20 minutes. Remove and serve on a pretty platter. Garnish with cherry tomatoes and parsley sprigs.

Note: You can use many combinations of vegetables for this dish. Add any herbs you want along with rice, mixed vegetables or elbow macaroni. Zucchini shells are imaginative and easy. It's a great luncheon dish, or cut into thirds, it's a tasty hot or cold appetizer!

SHAFT BITES

Serves 6-8

This delectable trio of bite-size morsels fills your mouth with several flavors and makes eating a pleasure. I think most people serve only one vegetable for most recipes. They are really adventurous when using two, and if three or more... **well, throw me down and spread me out!!** I always think of variety! Using three or more for flavor and esthetics makes sense. <u>Try using several vegetables together.</u>

1 bunch of broccoli - washed, trimmed, and cut into 1-1/2 inch flowerets. (I use some of the stem. Cut into smaller pieces. Make a few slits in them. There is no reason why you have to throw all the stems away, especially when you are using several other vegetables.)

4-6 large carrots, pared and cut diagonally into 1 inch pieces
8 oz. small white onions (frozen are real good for this part of the dish - less work).
2 cloves garlic, minced
2 tablespoons olive oil plus 2 tablespoons water or white wine
1 tablespoon pepper
1 tablespoon parsley

Garnish: lemon wedges, hard-boiled grated egg whites, grated romano cheese.

Optional: 1 teaspoon dill or fennel, rosemary, basil, thyme. Any of these herbs change the flavor.

In a large saucepan, steam broccoli in 2 inches of water for 7-9 minutes. Drain. While broccoli is cooking, in a large frying pan, saute' carrots in olive oil and garlic, stirring occasionally for about 10 minutes. Add onions, broccoli, pepper, parsley, and any other herbs. Add more water, if necessary. Cook until all vegetables are tender. If using a wok or frozen vegetables, the cooking times will vary.

Remove to serving dish. Sprinkle with grated hard-boiled egg whites or grated romano cheese. Add lemon wedges.

<u>OTHER COMBINATIONS:</u>

A. Carrots, yellow and green squash, and onions.
B. Broccoli, artichoke bottoms, large mushroom caps, and onions.

Note: Add more olive oil, water, wine, or lemon juice if extra liquid is needed in the frying pan.

SPOTTED DICK

Serves 8

This recipe can be used as an appetizer, luncheon dish, or main vegetable. Every culture has a name for it. Every Mediterranean country has a special way to make it. But, No One calls it "SPOTTED DICK"!! IT'S ALL MINE! Ratatouille - the way it was meant to be!! Big chunks of eggplant and black olives. If you ever see a "Dick" like THIS one, run fast! It's probably been out too long!

Ingredients:

1 medium eggplant, washed well. Remove ends. Partially peel. Leave some skin on it
    about every inch or so as you go along.
2 medium zucchini, cut into 1/2 inch pieces
1 large onion, cut into large chunks
1 large tomato, cut into pieces
1 green pepper, seeded and cut into chunks
1 red pepper, seeded and cut into chunks
3 cloves garlic, minced
1 tablespoon Burgundy wine or red cooking wine
1 (8 oz.) can tomato sauce
1/2 cup sliced mushrooms
1/2 cup black olives - pitted, whole
1 tablespoon black pepper
1 tablespoon Italian herbs or 1 teaspoon each oregano, thyme, and basil
1/2 teaspoon crushed red pepper flakes
1/4 cup fresh chopped parsley

Optional: 1 tablespoon chopped capers; (these add a little salt flavor).

Are you exhausted from chopping? Then lie down and make it later! This recipe makes up quite a bit.

In a **very large** saucepan or a Dutch oven, add all the ingredients. The preparation is a killer, but all you have to do is bring the mixture to a boil, stir occasionally, and simmer for 45 minutes, covered. Adjust seasonings to suit your taste. Serve in a soup tureen or deep bowl.

Note: Two things to remember.... Stir it occasionally, because you do not want the vegetables to scorch; and, if there is too much liquid, drain off some in a colander when the dish is finished. It is the flavor you want, not the liquid.

SUGGESTION: When you make up a large amount, you can refrigerate it and reheat whenever you get hungry. Ratatouille can be chopped up in the food processor. It then makes a great relish or spread on Italian bread, rice cakes, pita, or melba crackers.

MUFFALETTA

Serves 8

Do not confuse this recipe with the famous New Orleans sandwich. This vegetable/ noodle pudding is moist, cheesy, and loaded with tasty apples and raisins. **Once you have stuck your face into this dish, no other muffaletta will compare!**

Ingredients:

1 lb. (16 oz.) package egg noodles. Prepare according to directions. Drain, and rinse in cold water.
1 small onion, finely chopped
1 clove garlic, minced
1/2 cup fresh chopped parsley
1 cup grated Granny Smith apples or red delicious apples
1/2 cup golden raisins
1/2 cup (1% milk fat) cottage cheese
1 egg, plus 1 egg white
1/2 cup non-fat plain yogurt
1 tablespoon black pepper
2 tablespoons melted butter

Preheat oven to 375 degrees

In a large bowl, mix noodles with all the other ingredients. Spray a large 2-1/2 quart casserole dish with non-stick cooking spray. Bake, uncovered, for 30-45 minutes until top is golden brown. This dish should sit covered with foil for 10-15 minutes before serving. If you make this in a 13 x 9 inch dish, you may have to cut the baking time down 5 minutes.

You cannot ruin this recipe! If pudding looks too thick, add a little skim milk. Cool and cut into squares. Sprinkle with cinnamon and almonds, if desired.

SUGGESTION: Want to get disgusting??! Spoon some cherry pie filling or apple pie filling and whipped topping over the top. Serve it as a dessert. It is also delicious cold. The next day enjoy it with a green salad and a chicken breast!

I told you my Muffaletta was good!

SCHMUCKS

Guess what this is? It starts out very <u>long</u> and hard, and ends up in smaller, softer pieces! They are full of Vitamin A and help you to see at night. <u>Maybe they will help you see your Schmuck at night!!</u>.... Sweet and Sour Carrots, Mushrooms and Peppers! **What a delightful treat!**

6-8 medium to large carrots, peeled and cut diagonally into 1 inch pieces.
2 green peppers, seeded and cut into chunks
1 large onion, cut into wedges
1 pound large mushrooms - use mostly the caps. Cut into large pieces or leave whole.
2 cloves garlic, minced
1 tablespoon black pepper
1 bottle of sweet and sour dressing. Some sweet and sour dressings contain no fat.
    They are perfect for many recipes if you do not want to make your own up.

In a <u>very large</u> saucepan, steam carrots for 10 minutes in 2 inches of boiling water. Drain. Combine all the other ingredients in the saucepan. Cover and simmer for 30 minutes. Stir once or twice. Serve over rice or chicken.

If you are making your own sauce, combine:

8 ounces of tomato sauce
1 tablespoon Worcestershire sauce
1 teaspoon horseradish
1 tablespoon hot mustard
2 tablespoons vinegar
1 teaspoon garlic powder
1 teaspoon sugar substitute

Note: Change ingredients to suit your taste. Cook vegetables in the dressing and you'll see that it's similar to a carrot ratatouille!

SUGGESTION: If you do not want to make this recipe in a saucepan, you can saute' it for 15 minutes in a large frying pan or for 5 minutes in a wok. It is the combination of carrots and other vegetables in a sweet and sour sauce that makes this delicious.

I give you suggestions for combination cooking. You cannot go wrong with most of the things I suggest! It is my way of teaching you to use imagination!

<u>(And you are doing s-o-o good!)</u>

THE GRINDER

Serves 8

This is the **"BIG ONE!"**. More than a mouthful! Make it as a meatless vegetable. Add your favorite ground beef or ground turkey and you have a main meal that will fill up the best of cavities. Remember, you made it here first! <u>My grinders are the talk of the town</u>

There are a lot of ingredients in this recipe and it takes a little longer to prepare, but you can make it ahead of time, freeze it, and serve when needed.

1 large head of cabbage or 2 medium heads. You want to be sure of enough large
     outer leaves.
1 large onion, chopped
1 small carrot, grated
2 cloves garlic, minced
2 tablespoons vegetable oil; or 1 tablespoon butter and 1 tablespoon oil
2 cups cooked brown or white rice
1 large tomato, chopped
1 tablespoon fresh lemon juice
1 tablespoon black pepper

Garnish: parsley sprigs and cherry tomatoes

<u>Sauce:</u>

Combine the following in a bowl:

3 tablespoons tomato paste
1 cup tomato juice - low-salt variety
1/2 cup low-salt canned beef bouillon; or 1 package low-sodium beef bouillon, dissolved
     in 1/2 cup water.
1 cup raisins
1/2 tablespoon cinnamon, optional

Note: If you use meat, saute' until browned; drain off the fat and add to the rice mixture.

Wash the head of cabbage. Core the cabbage any way you can. (It's not always easy!). In a large saucepan, steam the cabbage for 10 minutes or until leaves are pliable. Drain and peel off 16 large leaves or use the smaller ones and make more. You may want to use 2 cabbages and save the remaining leaves for my Chew Me Coleslaw.

continued on next page...

Preheat oven to 375 degrees

In a large frying pan, saute' carrot, onion and garlic in oil for 5 minutes. In a large bowl, combine rice, tomatoes, seasonings and onion-carrot mixture. Shred some extra cabbage for the bottom of the casserole (about 2 cups or more).

Take a large cabbage leaf and place 2 tablespoons of rice mixture inside the leaf. Fold up, tucking in the sides and then roll up - securing the edges. Fasten with a toothpick (remember to take the toothpick out, or tell your guests it's in there! It could ruin a good night!)

Spray a large baking dish with non-stick cooking spray. Line the bottom with the extra grated cabbage. Place the cabbage rolls seam side down and pour the sauce over the cabbage rolls.

Bake, covered, in the oven for 1 hour. After 30 minutes, baste. Check to see that there is enough liquid. You do not want this dish to be dry. If more liquid is needed, add tomato juice and carefully mix it in. Transfer the rolls to a large serving platter. Garnish with parsley sprigs and cherry tomatoes. Serve extra sauce on the side.

Note: The carrot, rice and tomato filling is very good, but if beef is used, it does become more of a main meal. The extra cabbage and raisins in the casserole add much flavor and the sauce is light and very low in calories. This recipe can be made on top of the stove. Use a very large Dutch oven and simmer for 1 hour. Adjust cabbage rolls so they cook evenly.

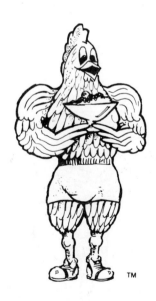

SNATCH A BATCH

Serves 6-8

My version of Succotash. Prepare a whole batch up! Serve cold as a relish with cold cuts, or use as a stuffing inside tomatoes and green pepper cups!

2 (8 oz.) cans or 2 packages of frozen corn
1 (8 oz.) can or 1 package of frozen lima beans
2 tablespoons butter - add water to butter if more liquid is necessary.
1 small onion, chopped
2 cloves garlic, minced
1/2 cup chopped green pepper
1 tablespoon chopped pimento
1 teaspoon black pepper
Onion powder to taste

Garnish: Grated Swiss cheese - optional

In a large frying pan, melt butter. Saute' green pepper, onion, garlic and pimento for several minutes until tender. Add the corn and lima beans. Adjust seasonings. Heat 10-15 minutes or until well blended. Stir occasionally. Serve in a pretty bowl. Sprinkle with grated Swiss cheese.

What a snatch! Quite a batch!

SUGGESTION: This relish can also be stuffed inside a chicken or Horny Hen. Add extra bread cubes or crumbs and it's an unusual stuffing.

TM

POLYNESIAN PEA PEA PODS

Serves 6

This is one of the easiest vegetable dishes you can make. It is a **great** accompaniment for chicken and fish.

2 (8 oz.) packages frozen pea pods or 1 lb. fresh. If frozen, prepare as package directs.
    If fresh, wash, cut off tips, remove string and steam for 2-3 minutes.
2 tablespoons butter
1 tablespoon peanut oil
1/2 teaspoon sesame oil
1 can sliced water chestnuts, drained
1 can bamboo shoots, drained
1 can button mushrooms, drained
1 (16 oz.) can pineapple chunks, drained - reserve 2 tablespoons liquid
2 cloves garlic, minced

Garnish: cherry tomatoes & radishes

In a large frying pan or wok, saute' garlic in butter, oils and pineapple juice. Add all the other ingredients, including pea pods. Stir-fry for several minutes.

Transfer to a serving dish and garnish with cherry tomatoes or radishes.

SUGGESTION: After this vegetable dish is cooked, chill it. Add a can of tuna, chicken or turkey chunks and serve on lettuce leaves as a salad for lunch.

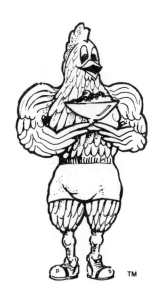

TITTY TOTS

Serves 6-8

This recipe starts out as whole "New" potatoes and ends up as a "Hot" potato salad that is a main dish in itself - just like you!

2 pounds new potatoes - (not too large) washed. Leave the skin on.
1/2 cup grated hard-boiled egg whites - about 4 eggs
2 cloves garlic, minced
1 small sweet onion, chopped
1 small head of Iceberg, Curly Endive, and Romaine lettuce torn into small pieces. A combination of greens is pretty and appetizing.
1 cup smoked turkey breast, turkey pastrami, or turkey ham - cut into small strips

Dressing:

1/2 cup vinegar - wine, garlic, tarragon, etc.
1 teaspoon black pepper
1 teaspoon celery seed
1 teaspoon Dijon mustard

Garnish: 1/2 cup chopped scallions and 1/2 cup sliced radishes

In a large Dutch oven or kettle, boil the titty tots. 30 - 40 minutes is usually sufficient. Let cool and cut into large pieces. In a serving bowl, toss the potatoes with egg whites, garlic, onion, and greens. Heat dressing and simmer for 2 minutes. Pour over potato salad. Toss. Add smoked turkey. Garnish with scallions and radishes. You can mix the turkey into the potato salad, but I like to layer it on the top. **Serve Hot!**

This is a basic new potato salad recipe. Use any dressing you like.

SUGGESTION: Substitutions for Turkey Cold Cuts

Chicken, tuna, salmon, smoked fish, large shrimp or seafood blend.

THE CROWN JEWELS

Serves 6-8

I hope you will NEVER see "jewels" like these! They are small, green, and in a sauce! You might see them small, or maybe even green, but in a sauce?? **HEAVEN FORBID!**

This recipe is about one of the most maligned vegetables of all times. It brings a "yuck" or a look of disgust to children and can cause grown men to hover in their tracks. **Someday people will really use these gems the way they were meant to be used!** I **eat them constantly and love them. Can you guess? BRUSSELS SPROUTS!** (good for you!) Two servings to the genius!

1 pound of fresh Brussels sprouts - cleaned, washed, and ready to steam. If using frozen sprouts, use 2 (10 oz.) packages and cook according to directions.

1/4 cup chopped onion
1/2 cup sliced mushrooms
2 cloves garlic, minced
1/2 teaspoon black pepper
1 tablespoon butter
1/4 cup hard-boiled egg whites, grated (about 2-3 eggs)

In a large non-stick frying pan, melt butter and add enough water to just cover the bottom of the pan. Saute' onion, mushrooms, garlic and pepper. Cook several minutes, just until tender. Turn off heat. In a large saucepan, cook Brussels sprouts in a steamer basket about 10-15 minutes until tender. Allow to cool. Cut sprouts in half and add to the other ingredients in the frying pan. Stir until heated through.

Place mixture on a serving platter or bowl and garnish with grated egg whites.

SUGGESTION: 1/4 teaspoon dry mustard, 1 tablespoon chopped parsley and 1/4 cup non-fat plain yogurt can also be added to the mixture for a creamy and more seasoned version.

Note: You do not have to cut your sprouts, but they go farther. If for some reason they are not tender, it won't seem so traumatic. They will be half as difficult to chew! I like to add other condiments to the basic sauce. But, no matter what you do to a sprout, I always say, "it still always tastes like a sprout!".

GIVE ME HEAD CHEESE

Serves 6-8

So, you think that you are cute, pretty smart, and feeling pretty cocky?! **Well, you aren't!** I can insult you because this one was even difficult for <u>me</u> to do.

<u>MY</u> head is cauliflower and <u>MY</u> cheese is melted and hot. How's your head and cheese? This is a beautiful way to serve a perfect vegetable that is quite as unique as you.

1 large head of cauliflower - cleaned and washed. Leave whole.
2 tablespoons butter
1 teaspoon black pepper
1 teaspoon dry mustard
1 tablespoon fresh chopped parsley
1 tablespoon fresh chopped garlic
1/4 cup sweet onion, chopped
1/4 cup hard-boiled egg whites, grated (about 2-3 eggs)
1/2 cup sliced mushrooms - canned is okay for this, but you could use fresh, (slice thin).
1/4 cup low-fat, reduced-calorie Swiss cheese, grated
1/4 cup fresh romano cheese, grated

Note: I like to use both cheeses for this recipe. It gives the cauliflower great color and taste. (1/4 cup any reduced-fat, lower calorie-cheese may be used).

Place a steamer basket in a large saucepan or pot. Add about 2-3 inches of water and bring to a rapid boil. Add the whole head of cauliflower. Reduce to simmer. Cover and steam for 20-25 minutes. A steamer basket works great because the head is held in place and it cooks evenly.

In a large frying pan, saute' all the other ingredients, except the egg whites and cheeses, in the butter. Cook for 5 minutes. Drain cauliflower and place in a large, pretty glass bowl. Pour on butter sauce. Sprinkle with egg whites and cheeses. Add a little extra parsley and black pepper. Cut into wedges or break apart. **Get Into it!**

SUGGESTION: This dish also looks pretty when surrounded with cherry tomatoes and radish roses. Again, you can change some ingredients to suit your own taste. I add more garlic, pepper, and scallions. If you want to use extra mushrooms make sure they are cooked. If you use extra cheese, you may want to stir the cheese into the sauce. The entire picture is elegant!

COCK RINGS

Serves 8

This could be the best recipe of the lot.! It is beautiful, tasty, and can be used as a vegetable on your antipasto platter, a relish, a side salad, or main salad if incorporated with chicken, turkey or tuna.

And _what_ a name! "Come on over to my house. I'm making Cock Rings!" Bet your Mama never said _that_ to dear old Dad! Maybe she should have! Spice in a relationship is healthy. Well, are you ready to find out what this is? No. No. It's not that! You **ARE** beginning to understand this book!

It's a marinated, multi-colored pepper ring salad, in an olive oil, basil, garlic, and vinaigrette dressing. I told you in the beginning that a mind is an incredible thing to waste. **THIS** mind is a nightmare!

Here goes!

9 assorted large peppers - 3 green, 3 red, 3 yellow, washed
1 large Vidalia or Spanish onion
4 cloves garlic - too much? Mrs. Boner likes garlic.
1/2 cup olive oil
1 tablespoon Balsamic vinegar
1 teaspoon basil
Black pepper to taste

Garnish: egg slices, cherry tomatoes, radish roses

Optional: 1 teaspoon Dijon mustard for a Dijon vinaigrette dressing

Note: Cut down on the garlic if you want to breath on your man or lady and have them come back!

Cut the peppers into 1/2 inch slices. Then cut around the membrane and scoop out the seeds. This keeps the rings intact. Thinly slice the onion. Mince garlic. Combine the vegetables and garlic in a large deep bowl.

Mix olive oil, vinegar, basil and pepper. Add the dressing to the pepper rings. Cover and refrigerate several hours or overnight. Stir occasionally. Before serving, drain the peppers.

Serve on a bed of Romaine, spinach or any combination of greens. Garnish with egg slices, radish roses or cherry tomatoes.

SUGGESTION: As a cold pasta dish, serve the peppers over the pasta of your choice. Add chunk tuna or large pieces of chicken. But I like this as a side dish and served just on lettuce. The garlic and olive oil makes the flavors of the three peppers so fantastic. No cock rings were ever THIS good! They will never forget you.

Desserts, Plus...
(Afterglow!!)

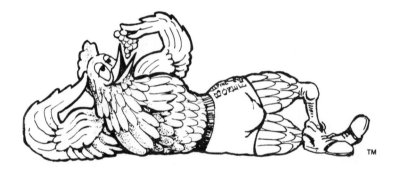

CUNT CANDY

Serves 1 orgy nicely, or 2 small gang bangs!

Makes about 1 pound.

The cherries in this recipe make it "oh so wholesome and pure!" Men will come back for MORE of this heavenly creamy fudge. Close your eyes and try to remember the good old days. As healthy as I would like to think my body is, I'm only human. <u>Just have him work it off you!</u>

2/3 cup milk
1-1/2 cups sugar
3 tablespoons butter
1 teaspoon vanilla
4 oz. white chocolate
8 oz. semi-sweet chocolate pieces
1/4 cup chopped pecans
1/4 cup chopped candied cherries

In a large saucepan, combine milk and sugar. Bring to a full boil; reduce heat, simmer and stir constantly for 3 minutes until well blended.

Remove from heat and stir in white chocolate, butter and vanilla. Fold in chocolate chips, nuts and cherries.

Pour into a buttered 8 or 9 inch pan. Cool. Refrigerate. Cut into squares.

SUGGESTION: If you don't like this fudge cold, then <u>eat it out of the pot HOT!</u>

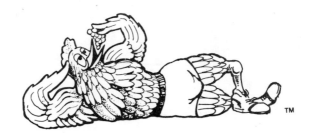

BLOOMER PUDDING

Serves 4

This creamy golden confection is easy to make and easy to eat. If you don't like it in the dessert glasses, you'll love it on your guests!!

1 package sugar-free banana instant pudding
1 large, ripe banana - diced
1-1/2 cups miniature marshmallows
2 tablespoons chopped maraschino cherries
Non-dairy whipped topping
Chopped pecans

Prepare pudding according to package directions. Stir in bananas, marshmallows, and cherries. Save a few extra cherries for the top. Spoon into parfait glasses. Top with dessert topping, nuts and cherries.

SUBSTITUTIONS FOR BANANA PUDDING: Sugar-free vanilla, chocolate or butterscotch.

MASTERBAKE

1 Loaf

How about cornbread? It is very nutritious and easy to make. A master baker could NOT make it better than you could!

1-3/4 cups cornmeal
1-1/2 cups all-purpose flour
1/2 cup wheat germ
1/3 cup sugar
1-1/2 teaspoons salt
1 teaspoon baking powder
2 cups buttermilk
1/2 cup vegetable oil
2 eggs, beaten slightly

Preheat oven to 375 degrees. Lightly grease a 9 x 5 inch loaf pan.

Mix all the dry ingredients in a large bowl. Mix thoroughly. In a smaller bowl, mix buttermilk and oil with eggs. Blend liquid mixture into dry ingredients and mix just until moistened. Do not over mix. Keep the mixture lumpy. Pour immediately into pan. Bake 1 hour until golden brown and done. Cool 10-15 minutes and transfer to wire rack.

*SUGGESTION: Add 1 tablespoon chopped jalapenos to batter. **A GREAT MEXICAN CORN BREAD!***

BLOW MY BLUEBERRIES BABY

Serves 6-8

You may want to blow your baby's apples, peaches, apricots, pears or any of his or hers assorted fruits you select! This fruit crisp is like fruit oatmeal. <u>If you don't want it for dessert, why not instant breakfast in bed!</u>

4 cups fresh blueberries, or 2 cans drained blueberries
1/3 cup water
Juice of 1 lemon
4-6 tablespoons melted butter or margarine. It's a dessert for 8. It's not THAT bad!
1/2 cup wheat germ
1/2 cup low-calorie light brown sugar, 25% reduced-calorie
1-1/4 cups dry oatmeal
1 tablespoon cinnamon
Dash of nutmeg

Preheat oven to 375 degrees

Spray a 13 x 9 inch baking dish with non-stick cooking spray. Place berries in baking dish. In a small bowl, mix water and lemon juice. In another bowl, mix all the other ingredients and add the liquid. Mix until crumbly. Sprinkle evenly over fruit. Bake for 30-35 minutes. If mixture looks a little dry, add more water. Sprinkle with cinnamon and nutmeg. Cool. Serve with creams. **That sounds good! Creams! Ice cream, whipped cream... YOUR cream!!**

Note: I like to spoon this treat into sherbert or parfait glasses. Layer with whipped topping. <u>It tastes like a rich, sweet dessert.</u>

For apples use Granny Smiths, Rome Beauties, Red Delicious, or Northern Spys. You need a firmer baking apple. You can use any pie filling and change any of the dry ingredients to suit your taste. Flour can be used instead of the wheat germ.

SUGGESTION: Who said crisps and cobblers had to be dessert? Egg whites and blueberry crisp! I think that this is a perfect breakfast. Oatmeal, fruit and wheat germ. Real healthy, huh?

PUT YOUR BANANA IN AND OUT

Serves 4

1 Banana per person (what else?). You do NOT want to share your banana!!

4 Bananas

Extra added attractions:

nuts, fruit juice, chocolate syrup, granola, coconut, peanut butter, melted caramels... need I say more? What you put on your banana, you get out of it!

Popsicle sticks

This is really tough, so put those brain caps on and get your act together!

Cut the bananas in half. Insert (**ANOTHER great word!**) a popsicle stick in each half.

Cut waxed paper and place it on a baking sheet. Roll your banana in fruit juice, then in coconut, chocolate and granola, peanut butter and chocolate. (This is where we separate the adults from the kids). Your imagination can be incredible! ANY combination is fine - from simple to sinful!

Freeze. **In approximately 2 hours you can "suck" your hearts out! Yummy and nutritious too!**

SUGGESTION: I like to take a cup of chocolate, melt the caramels, add nuts, granola, peanut butter and coconut and **FORGET THE BANANA!** Just use a spoon and don't have any regrets in the morning!

Note: This treat will probably be better than your date. Bananas are so rich in potassium and so economical, that just frozen by themselves, they are delicious! There should be a class taught in the art of "eating" a banana. Maybe in a book to come, Mrs. Boner will give some advice on how to "get your banana off"!

DEEP THROAT APPLE PIE

Serve 6-8

This one has you buzzing, I'll bet! Apple Betty has a new twist... A banana! That's why this traditional dessert is made customized for you with firm bananas incorporated into it. Get it?? Deep Throat!!

2 large Granny Smith apples - pared, cored and thinly sliced
3 firm, medium yellow bananas, cut into 1/2 inch slices
    (dip in lemon juice to prevent browning)
1/2 cup low-calorie light brown sugar - 25% reduced-calorie
1 tablespoon cinnamon
1 tablespoon lemon juice
3 cups soft bread crumbs. Italian bread is good for this one.
4 tablespoons melted butter or margarine
(You may need to add more water)

Preheat oven to 375 degrees

In a large bowl, combine fruits with sugar, cinnamon and lemon juice. Grease an 8 or 9 inch baking dish or any 2-quart casserole dish. You can spray with non-stick cooking spray. In another bowl, combine crumbs with butter. Start with a crumb layer, then fruit, crumbs, etc., ending with fruit. Sprinkle crumbs over top, but don't make a heavy layer. Bake covered for 40 minutes. If mixture is dry, add a little water. Uncover and bake 5 minutes longer until crumbs are browned.

Serve warm with yogurt or whipped topping. This sure is different! Enjoy! Sweet AND tart!

SUGGESTION: You can use whole wheat bread crumbs, but I think this may even taste too healthy for me! Try oatmeal and you have another crisp, but with apples and bananas.

Note: You may have to "play" with the size of the baking dish, but you do want two layers of fruit.

BEAVER JAM

Yields 1-1/2 - 2 cups

This spoon on spread is so simple, you will make it up regularly. Serve it over waffles, French toast, muffins, tea breads, fresh fruit salads, **or your beaver!**

1 cup (1% milkfat) small curd cottage cheese, or 8 oz. Neufchatel cream cheese; or use a blend of 1/2 cup yogurt and 1/2 cup cream cheese - any combination of the above.

1/2 - 1 cup chopped fruit (bananas, apples, peaches, pineapple, etc.)

.Sprinkle on or add: brown sugar, cinnamon, nutmeg, coconut, raisins, dates, chocolate chips.

SUGGESTION: Canned fruits can be used, but drain well. In a food processor, whip fruit with cheese. I like peaches whipped with cream cheese. Yogurts make this jam a little more watery and I like a thicker spread. Apricots, bananas, and Granny Smith apples make a great spread. Just chop fruit and blend. Serve on anything. REAL EASY!

WHIPPED CREAM WITH UTTER DELIGHTS

Serves 8

"Utterly" delicious!! Baked apples with honey and cinnamon. This one is for the calorie conscious.

8 Granny Smith apples, or large red delicious, or ANY baking apple
1 cup water
1/2 cup apple juice concentrate
1/4 cup honey
2 tablespoons cinnamon
Whipped cream or ice cream; non-dairy whipped topping or ice milk

Preheat oven to 350 degrees

Line a 13 x 9 inch baking pan with foil. Wash, core and remove skin (1/3 way down) on the apples. Mix water and all other ingredients, except topping, in a bowl. Place apples in baking pan. Pour liquid over apples and make sure it gets into the center. Cover and bake for 30 minutes. Uncover and baste. Cover and bake 30 minutes longer. Baste before serving.

Top with whatever you want! Baked apples are a great last minute dessert, or if cold, they are SO GOOD with pound cake or ice cream.

Note: I like them cold the next day as a snack!

TASTE MY CUMQUATS

Serves 8

This very fresh and sweet fruit medley is fantastic after a spicy meal. If fresh fruits are not in season, you can use canned ones. **It is definitely a great change from your traditional fruit cup.**

1 (20 oz.) can pitted, whole lychees (reserve 1/2 cup syrup)
1/2 cup orange marmalade, low-sugar variety
1/2 teaspoon fresh grated ginger root, or a piece of preserved ginger, or a teaspoon of
    candied ginger
1 (20 oz.) can whole pitted loquats, drained
1 (20 oz.) can pineapple chunks, drained
1 large can mandarin orange sections, drained

Garnish: maraschino cherries or currants

Optional: 4 kiwi fruit, 2 cups green seedless grapes, persimmons, fresh kumquats. (They are heavy and very sweet - resembling pecans.) I like to add 1 cup of them to the recipe, but they are very rich. Keep this mixture sweet. That is the purpose.

Drain lychees, reserve 1/2 cup syrup, and cut in half. Combine syrup, marmalade, and ginger. In a serving bowl, combine all fruits. Drizzle liquid over fruit. Stir occasionally and chill at least 4 hours. Stir gently.

Note: This is beautiful in pineapple boats, melon halves, or in dessert glasses. The "cumquats" can be cut in half and served with a soft cream cheese or yogurt.

SUGGESTION: If you drain this dessert thoroughly, it is <u>delicious</u> over Pound-Me Cake., See recipe.

TWATTY'S TORTE

Serves 8-10

Please do not get crazy with this one. It is easy..don't freak! When you serve this, the men will be on their knees crawling back for more!! Just say "NO"! (You are watching their waistlines!)

1 box of fudge; or double fudge; or chocolate cake mix (get the hint? We want chocolate)!
1 can ready to spread chocolate fudge; or Dutch chocolate fudge frosting (Oh No! more chocolate!)
1 package frozen bing cherries, defrosted and drained well. Make sure there are no pits in there. They do sometimes slip in and you do not want one of your dates to break a tooth - **bad ending!**
1 tablespoon almond, coffee, or chocolate cherry liqueur
2 tablespoons chocolate chips, 1 tablespoon almonds or pecans, and maraschino cherries.

Prepare cake mix as package directs. Cool for several hours. Cut each layer into two layers. When finished, you have 4 layers for your torte. For easy cutting, use a sharp knife, bend down level with the cake and carefully cut through each layer making two layers. You can put toothpicks around the layers as a guide to cut around, but I think it's too much work!

Squeeze all the extra juice out of the cherries in paper towels. Stir the cherries into the frosting. Add the liqueur and 1 tablespoon of chocolate chips.

Spread the frosting between the layers and on the top. Sprinkle the top layer with 1 tablespoon chocolate chips, 1 tablespoon pecans or almonds and several maraschino cherries. Cover loosely with plastic wrap and store in the refrigerator. Remove 1 hour before serving.

Close your eyes... see the flavors mixing together. Can you imagine it! Four layers of chocolate cake, sandwiching a rich spread of cherries and liqueur in fudge frosting. Yummy! Go to it!

Note: If you think that he/she is worth a second piece, send them out for a good chocolate ice cream and you can eat till you croak... Mrs. Boner's "Death by Chocolate!" Maybe they will think you are a French Bakery... tell them you are a French tart!. **Make them beg for mercy!**

THROW ME DOWN AND FUCK ME FUDGE

I think this recipe is self-explanatory. It is not healthy, nor low-calorie. It isn't even good for you! It snuck into this book! It is guaranteed to do just what the name says. It's addicting! It's easy! It makes so much you think it is "growing" in the container! **Good luck and Boner Appetite!™**

Dedicated to my dear friend, Roz, who is doing more in the bedroom than in the kitchen! But then, I'm the one writing the book. One day she shrieked out this name in a frenzy, broke out in a sweat, and - three pounds of fudge later - THIS ONE'S FOR YOU, ROZ!

Makes 3 pounds, or enough to give anyone that high they have always dreamed of and the thighs they'll want to cut off.

Use a 13 x 9 inch baking pan greased with a small amount of butter.

2-1/2 cups sugar
1 stick butter
2/3 cup evaporated milk
2 (8 oz.) packages semi-sweet chocolate pieces
4 cups miniature marshmallows
1 cup chopped cashews or pecans
1-1/2 teaspoons vanilla

In a large saucepan, combine milk, butter and sugar. Cook and stir till mixture comes to a rapid boil. Reduce heat and simmer, stirring constantly, for 5 minutes. Remove from heat and stir in chocolate until blended. Add all the other ingredients. Pour into prepared pan and chill several hours. This freezes well. When cold, it cuts easily and breaks apart into odd-shaped chocolate chunks.

SUGGESTION:

Extra Treats: *Peanut butter chips, shredded coconut, raisins, peanuts, whole almonds.*

FUZZY NAVELS

Serves 8

No... this is NOT the drink that you can guzzle down and get sloshed on! **Not in THIS health book!** But, the Fuzzy is coconut and the navels are oranges. It is a frozen orange sherbert dessert that is very light and extremely pretty.

Graham cracker crumbs, ginger snap crumbs, or vanilla wafer crumbs
1 quart orange sherbert, softened
2 cans mandarin orange sections, drained
8 oz. non-dairy whipped topping
1/2 cup coconut, shredded
Miniature marshmallows
Maraschino cherries, halved

Note: If you are a "snacking cookie eater", then you might want to stay with graham crackers, ginger snaps or fruit Newtons. They are the safer ones. They DO have some fat and sugar, but much less then other cookies. Make your crumbs up and store them in the freezer. You then have them for baking, sprinkling on other foods, over yogurts or fruits, etc.

Use a 9 inch round pie plate or a 9 x 5 inch loaf pan. Line loaf pan with wax paper and spray with cooking spray. This will help the dessert come out easier.

Sprinkle a fine layer of crumbs on the bottom of prepared dish. Let sherbert soften. Spread a 1 inch layer over the crumbs. (Coat your serving spoon with spray and sherbert won't stick). Freeze for 1/2 hour. Layer 1 inch of whipped topping over the sherbert. Evenly distribute some orange sections, covering the topping. Sprinkle with coconut.

Freeze again for one hour. Layer another inch of sherbert, topping, and oranges. End with the coconut topping. Cover with plastic wrap and refreeze several hours. Make this a day ahead of time. When ready to serve, unmold, cut, and sprinkle with marshmallows and maraschino cherries. It looks beautiful! You should have at least 2 layers of sherbert, topping, oranges, etc. VERY COLORFUL!

*Note: I like making this dessert in sections because I don't want the layers to blend together. You can also use any assorted sherberts or fruits - from lime green with Kiwi fruit, to lemon, or rainbow with bananas. It's the layering with the topping and coconut that makes it look like a very expensive torte, but it is so **low-calorie and s-o-o-o easy!***

SUGGESTION: Spoon some orange marmalade or low-calorie jellies over the topping or fruit. It is sweet and looks pretty when cut. Low-sugar preserves dress up many cakes, pies, and tortes.

THREE-SOME COOKIES

Makes about 3 dozen

These are three some and <u>then</u> some! Made with rolled oats, raisins, coconut AND zucchini. In fact, I should have put these in the vegetable category... zucchini cookies and Lay Sagna! <u>Lots of ingredients and lots of flavor!</u>

1-1/2 cups oatmeal (dry)
1-1/2 cups whole-wheat flour
2/3 cup chopped dates or raisins. I'll use raisins in this recipe.
1/2 cup coconut (flaked)
1-1/2 teaspoons cinnamon
1/2 teaspoon baking powder
1 stick butter
2/3 cup light brown sugar - 25% reduced-calorie
1 teaspoon vanilla
2 egg whites
2/3 cup grated zucchini

Preheat oven to 375 degrees

In a large bowl, mix oatmeal, whole wheat flour, raisins, coconut, cinnamon, and baking powder. In another bowl, blend butter, sugar, egg whites and vanilla. Stir in the dry ingredients and zucchini. Mix thoroughly.

Lightly oil your baking sheets. Drop mixture by rounded teaspoons about 2 inches apart on the sheets. Bake 10-12 minutes or until well browned. Remove to wire racks and cool. Store in covered containers.

*Note: These are little zucchini ball cookies. **Easy! Fun!** And **Delicious!** I don't like using the butter, but for 36 cookies these are not too fattening. They make a nice gift when you want something in return!*

GANG BANG MERINGUE PIE

Serves 8

The Gang! The Bang! The Meringue! <u>THEY'RE ALL TOGETHER</u>! But, there's more to this Gang Bang than meets the eye! This is NOT a simple lemon meringue gang bang pie... it's a lemon-lime mousse. **Two gangs for the price of one!!** One stop shopping for this lemon and lime mousse.

2 envelopes unflavored gelatin
1/4 cup cold water
1/4 cup fresh lemon juice
1 cup boiling water
1 cup lime sherbert
1 cup lemon sherbert
1 cup non-dairy whipped topping
Grated lemon and lime rinds
Fruits - frozen in syrup, or fresh - mixed with extra topping

In a large bowl, mix gelatin and lemon juice with cold water. Add boiling water and stir until well mixed and gelatin is dissolved. Gradually add sherberts, then whipped topping. Pour into a serving dish or individual dessert glasses. If served from a pie plate (great for a group gang dessert!), spoon it out and top with additional whipped topping and grated lemon and lime rinds. Chill several hours.

Serve with frozen strawberries, blueberries or raspberries. You can substitute **ANY** flavor of sherbert and use a variety of "berries".

SUGGESTION: You can make this dessert into a real pie by pouring the gelatin mixture over vanilla wafers, graham cracker crumbs, macaroon crumbs, or lady fingers. Press any one of these cookie bases into a pie plate and pour mixture over it. Chill several hours.

TM

MOON PIE or MACAROON ME

Serves 6-8

A cold souffle' and a hearty molded dessert that can be changed to "moon" anyone!!

1 quart vanilla ice milk (chocolate, coffee, strawberry, etc.). Any flavor can be
    substituted.
3 chocolate, almond, or coconut candy bars broken up
1 (oz.) almond flavored liqueur
1 cup non-dairy whipped topping

Line a 6-cup mold with plastic wrap. In a large bowl, soften ice milk and stir in crumbled
candy bars, liqueur, and whipped topping. Mrs. Boner likes chocolate ice milk, chocolate
coconut candy, chocolate cherry liqueur, (but I used almond liqueur in this recipe), and
topping.

Pour into mold. You want to pack as much of the mixture in as possible. Cover and
freeze several hours or overnight. Unmold and serve with low-calorie chocolate syrup,
chopped cherries, or any frozen fruit, like strawberries.

*SUGGESTION: The same dessert can be made in different molds and shapes, and with
different flavors. For instance, chocolate ice milk, peanut-butter candy bars, chocolate
liqueur, and topped with chopped peanuts.*

EAT MY CHERRY, PLEASE!

Serves 8

I can't do low-calorie desserts well! But, if you have had a nutritious and low-fat dinner,
then shit... plunge head first into a good dessert! If this is the first dessert you have
made from my book, THEN EAT MY CHERRY, PLEASE!

1 package chocolate cake mix
1 can cherry pie filling
1/2 cup butter (1 stick)
Ice cream, ice milk, whipped topping
Optional: toppings like chopped nuts, fudge sauce or extra cherries

Preheat oven to 375 degrees

Spread pie filling in the bottom of a 9 x 9 inch baking pan. Sprinkle with dry cake mix.
Cut butter into 8 to 12 pats and dot evenly over cake mix. Bake for 35-40 minutes.

Let cool. Serve with ice cream, toppings, etc.

*Note: This is very easy and very rich. Use blueberry, apple, or any other pie filing with
white cake mix.*

KNIGHT STICK

Serves 8-10

Want a special dessert that is black and rich? Maybe this dessert is YOUR date for the night. Get it?

(Under-bake the brownies, and this is the best!)

1 package family size brownie mix
1 quart peppermint ice cream, vanilla bean ice cream or ice milk
1/2 cup crushed peppermint candies. Make them in the food processor.
1 cup chocolate pieces
1 cup miniature marshmallows

Whipped topping

Preheat oven to 350 degrees

Prepare brownie mix as package directs. Add chocolate chips and marshmallows. Pour into two eight inch baking pans. Bake 20-25 minutes. Under-bake it. That's the secret to ALL brownies! They taste more like a fudge cake than a brownie... Yum!

Cool and transfer to serving plates. Soften ice cream and add crushed candy. Spread 1 layer of cake with ice cream and top with second layer of cake.

Freeze until ready to serve. Let stand 10-15 minutes before serving. Sprinkle with extra candies and whipped topping.

A 2-layer brownie and peppermint ice cream cake!

MUFFED MUFFINS

Makes 12 Muffins

And, you are asking, how did we get this name?? Tell me. What comes to your mind when I say, "a moist, juicy center surrounded by a hot and tasty... baked good? A surprise center that you can get at with your finger or tongue? A burst of excitement as your mouth fills with this delectable treat?" **Who says that a muffin has to be boring. Are YOU boring?** Well, should your muffin be??

I feel that compared to bagels, pita, or other whole wheat baked goods, a muffin - even a non-muffed one - is still more fattening than I'd like it to be. But, for that special occasion, a midnight snack, or for the morning after, bring out the good stuff! AND, THIS RECIPE IS GOOD STUFF!

2-3 medium very ripe bananas, mashed
1/2 cup raisins - brown, golden, or currants
1/2 cup chopped nuts. Optional, but I like pecans.
Strawberry or peach jelly

Note: This is a basic muffin recipe that can be altered and stuffed to your pleasure!

1-3/4 cups unbleached flour. You may use whole-wheat, but sometimes the muffin will
     be dry.
1/4 cup sugar
2-1/2 teaspoons baking powder
1 egg, well beaten
3/4 cup skim milk
1/3 cup peanut or safflower oil
Baking cup wrappers - the colored ones look so pretty around the muffin. There are so
     many fun wrappers out.

Preheat oven to 400 degrees

In a large bowl, mix together bananas, raisins, and nuts. In a separate bowl, mix dry ingredients. Combine egg, oil and milk. Add all at once to dry ingredients. Add banana mixture. Blend until just mixed. Mixture will be thick. Fill paper lined muffin cups 1/3 full. Add 1 teaspoon jelly to center of muffin and then add 1/3 more muffin mixture. Bake for 20-25 minutes. Serve warm.

The "muff" in the middle is jelly. **Spread 'em good with extra jelly!**

SUBSTITUTIONS FOR BANANAS:: 1 apple, grated. Add some cinnamon and brown sugar; 1 cup blueberries - fresh, with grated lemon rind; peanut butter inside the apple-raisin muffin; 1 cup fresh cranberries.

BANG MY BISCUITS BABY

Makes 12 biscuits

Biscuits are baked goods that say, "I made this for you because you are special!" They are quick to make, have variety - from plain baking powder biscuits to pecan biscuits. They can be made up in a few minutes and eaten by themselves, and that, as we all know, is very hard to do. **Did you ever try to eat YOURSELF?!**

With a little warm honey and a good preserve, they make an easy Sunday breakfast in bed or a quick get-together dish for late Sunday "high tea". When is the last time you got high at tea time!? **These biscuits are very healthy and require no kneading - you may require kneading, but your biscuits won't!**

1 cup all-purpose flour
1 tablespoon baking powder
1/2 stick butter - room temperature
1/2 teaspoon salt
1 cup dry oatmeal
1/2 cup skim milk
1 egg, slightly beaten
3 tablespoons honey
Marmalade, fresh fruit

Preheat oven to 425 degrees

In a large bowl, mix flour, baking powder and butter. Add 1/2 teaspoon salt. Use a pastry cutter for the mixing. Cut shortening in until mixture is like course bread crumbs. Stir in oats. Combine milk, egg and honey all at once. Stir until mixture is moistened. Drop by spoonfuls onto a large greased baking sheet. Bake at 425 degrees for 8-10 minutes. Serve warm. These biscuits are the "drop" kind because they do not have to be rolled out. You do not have to use a cookie cutter on them. They look like an oatmeal cookie and are a great cold snack as well. In fact, I eat them all the time. They even fit in your pocketbook or your pants - take them along with you!

Note: If you want to knead the dough, you can. The biscuit gets a little fluffier. I like the look of these "roughed-up" beauties, and I'd rather be kneaded!

Serve with honey and orange marmalade or strawberry preserves. For those who don't give a damn about the calories, serve with... **BUTTER!**

SUGGESTIONS: Add a tablespoon of cinnamon and sugar to mixture; add grated lemon or orange rind; add 1/2 cup chopped pecans; top with brown sugar and coconut

FUCKWHEAT PANCAKES

8 Babies

You would have to live on Mars not to know what I mean by this recipe! Serve them with apple sauce, sprinkled with cinnamon, low-calorie blueberry pancake syrup, or low-calorie maple syrup.

3/4 cup buckwheat flour
1/4 cup whole-wheat flour
1/2 cup wheat bran
3 tablespoons light brown sugar - 25% reduced-calorie
1-3/4 teaspoons double-acting baking powder
1 egg, plus 2 egg whites, slightly beaten
3 tablespoons safflower, corn oil or peanut oil
skim milk (1% milkfat)

In a large bowl, mix all ingredients together. Add enough milk to make the batter the consistency of heavy cream. Oil griddle and spoon mixture on with a ladle. When holes appear on top of the pancake, turn. Brown the other side. **Make sure griddle is hot.** Top with condiments of your choice.

Note: These are not going to taste like traditional pancakes. They are "serious" and very healthy. If you do not like the consistency and flavor of them, get a good chocolate ice cream and some hot fudge. Mix together and layer between the pancakes. Spoon marshmallow cream over it all. Now you won't care about the pancakes!! (But, there goes the health bit!)

Note: I'm really trying to keep this book healthy. It ain't easy because the "grained" recipes are NOT what you are used to eating. However, That's life!. I don't make the rules. I just give you a few suggestions. Chocolate is foolproof. So is a pizza. Those are my final words of wisdom to you. "When all else fails........ choose chocolate and/ or pizza!

WHORETILLA CHIPS

A batch for a bunch!

Each tortilla cuts into 10 chips. I eat 10 chips, so let's do this for eight people.

10 chips per person; 8 tortillas

Preheat oven to 350 degrees

Spray a large baking sheet with non-stick cooking spray. Press the tortilla down on the baking sheet. Remove. Re-spray and turn tortilla over. Press again. Cut each tortilla into 10 wedges. Sprinkle with garlic or onion powder, if desired. I season my chips with chili and popcorn seasonings. It makes for a unique flavored chip.

Please chips back on baking sheet and bake for 15 minutes. Do as many batches as necessary. Serve warm in a large bowl with a red checked napkin. OLE'! Homemade whoretilla chips. **You whore, you!**

HAND JOBS

Makes about 36

You are going to need several "hand jobs" after you have eaten these! Macaroon fudge NEVER felt so good!

2 cups sugar
5 tablespoons cocoa
1 can (7-1/2 oz.) coconut, flaked
2 teaspoons vanilla
1 stick butter (1/2 cup)
1/2 cup low-fat skim milk (I'm a hypocrite)
1/2 cup chunky peanut butter
2 cups finely chopped tortilla chips. Do not use my recipe - buy them in the bag.

In a large saucepan, combine the sugar, butter, cocoa, and milk. Boil for 3-5 minutes stirring constantly. Add remaining ingredients. Mix thoroughly.

Here comes the hand job! Take this mixture in your hands and make balls. Drop your balls on waxed paper and let set. Your hands will get messy, so keep them moist with a little cooking spray.

Note: These "jobs" are a great and easy snack. Keep them covered in the refrigerator. I like to freeze them and let them melt in my mouth in the middle of the night!

A PRICK OT BREAD

Makes 1 loaf

This is a heavy bread. Most baked goods are not good for you, but for a healthy snack, or for a justified treat, it's okay to cheat once in a while! **This very serious tea-bread is delicious and makes a lovely gift for someone, as well.... after they have taken you shopping!!!**

2 cups whole-wheat flour
1/2 cup low-calorie light brown sugar - 25% reduced-calorie
1-1/2 teaspoons cinnamon
1/2 teaspoon salt
2 teaspoons baking soda
2 (16 oz.) cans apricots, drained.
1 egg plus 2 egg whites
1/4 cup vegetable oil
2 teaspoons vanilla
1/2 cup golden raisins

Note: You can use white flour if you know someone doesn't like a whole-wheat product.

Preheat oven to 350 degrees

Spray a 9 x 5 inch loaf tin. Mix all dry ingredients in a large bowl. In your food processor, puree' apricots. To this mixture add eggs, oil and vanilla. Add raisins and add this mixture to the dry ingredients. Mix well, but do not stir too much. Pour batter into loaf tin. Bake for 55 minutes. Remove and let cool for a few minutes.

If you want to flour your loaf pan, you can.

Note: I do not mix "tea" breads (that's what these little breads are called in "better circles") too much. I would rather have them lumpy. If you stir them too much they can be heavy and may not rise like they should. ***When I'm heavy, I don't rise like I should either!***

Serve with Beaver Jam.

GO DOWN ON ME MUNCH

Makes _too_ much!

THE SCENARIO: A date calls you up and asks, "Want to go camping?" YEAH! RIGHT ON! **When was the last time you went camping?** "I'd love to", you say. "I'll bring a snack." (you are the snack!) Who are you trying to kid?! Into the kitchen you go. Panting and racing around trying to fix a "grocery" size order of these goodies in no time flat! So - I suggest you use gallon plastic bags - that way you can stick your whole head in the bag and not get your hands dirty!

2 cups popcorn - unsalted preferred
2 cups bite-size shredded wheat cereal
2 cups bran-chex cereal
2 cups rice-chex cereal
1 cup raisins, chopped dates, or diced apricots
1/2 cup coconut, shredded
1 cup dry roasted cashews or peanuts
1 cup broken pretzel sticks - unsalted preferred
1 cup chocolate pieces - optional

There is nothing more to say! Add any additional seasonings you like: Chili powder, garlic and onion powders, salt-free popcorn, etc.

Combine all the ingredients and the spices in a **HUGE BOWL.** Mix thoroughly. Store in tightly sealed containers or zip lock bags. Then Baby... **"GO DOWN ON IT!"**

CHOCOLATE ORGASM

Serves "Hordes"

This dessert "explodes" with variety and possibilities. In fact, after I give you the ultimate, the peak, the climax of this recipe, I will give you as many combinations as there are positions to do it! This dessert can be made up a week in advance, can be changed four different ways, eaten anywhere, at anytime, requires no silverware and leaves no mess. READY? CHOCOLATE BASKETS FILLED WITH ROLLED ICE CREAM BALLS.

CHOCOLATE BASKETS

Line or spray 8 - 12 large muffin cups (or more... depending on how many are to be made.)

1 cup semi-sweet chocolate pieces
1/2 cup miniature marshmallows
1-1/2 cups corn flakes (that's the HEALTHY part - breakfast in a cup)
1/2 cup flaked coconut
1/2 cup chopped peanuts or pecans

On top of a double boiler, melt chocolate. With fork, combine remaining ingredients and mix thoroughly. Press mixture into the bottom and up the sides of the muffin cups. Place in freezer and cover with foil. They will keep indefinitely.

Note: Use butterscotch, chocolate,or peanut butter chips for variety. You have three DIFFERENT kinds of baskets.

If you do not want individual muffins, press mixture into a baking pan or pie shell and you have a base for a pie or cake. Also, you can roll this mixture and drop by tablespoons onto a baking sheet and freeze. Serve as a cookie or macaroon.

Are you ready for the second half of your orgasm? *Please turn the page gently...*

ROLLED ICE CREAM BALLS

USE YOUR FAVORITE ICE CREAM OR ICE MILK, LOW-FAT YOGURT (FROZEN), OR SHERBERT, OR ANY REDUCED-CALORIE FROZEN CONFECTION.

Scoop out your favorite flavors and roll into 2 1/2 inch balls. Here is the fun part:

The varieties: coconut, chopped peanuts, etc., chopped chocolate morsels, peanut butter chips, butterscotch chips, chocolate sprinkles, (all those pretty sprinkles in the baking section of the market), chopped dried fruit or raisins, graham or ginger snap crumbs, crushed peppermint candy, etc., etc. Freeze, covered, until ready to use.

Remove muffin cups from freezer several hours before serving. They need to warm up. You do not want anyone to break a tooth!. The flavors also get better when at room temperature.

Fill each cup with your rolled ball. Drizzle a low-cal dessert topping over each. Fudge, butterscotch, etc. There are many reduced, very low-calorie sugar toppings on the market. Also, jellies and marmalades are fantastic on the sherbert balls.

If making this dessert as a pie, spread your ice cream over cookie crust and top with whipped topping. Sprinkle on any of the above ingredients.

Note: The base is delicious. The ice cream is your choice. The flavors and variety are endless. It can be made up way in advance and it is not really that fattening because you can use reduced-calorie ingredients. They are pretty and tasty.

Did you do good again? You devil, you!

DOUCHE DELIGHT

An easy and de-lightful recipe! Fresh fruits mixed with yogurt and "lo-cal" brown sugar.

Serves 4-6

2 cups seedless grapes (green, black, red, or combination)
2 medium oranges, sectioned
2 bananas - cut into 1 inch chunks (dip into fresh lemon juice to prevent darkening)
1 cup strawberries, halved
1/2 cup orange juice
1/4 cup honey
1/4 cup light brown sugar - 25% reduced-calorie
1/4 cup coconut
1/2 cup non-fat plain yogurt

In a pretty glass serving bowl, combine all the fruits. In a separate bowl, combine the orange juice, honey, brown sugar, coconut, and yogurt. Pour the dressing over the fruit. Top with extra coconut. Spoon into pretty sherbert glasses.

SUBSTITUTIONS: Peaches, apples, cantaloupes, etc. Play around with any fruits you want. Also, you can use a low-fat fruit yogurt. There are many that have only 1 gram of fat per serving.

Note: If you want to get real cute with this one, serve it in a cantaloupe half or pineapple boat. It is elegant and very tropical.

SPERMONI

Serves 8

Italians DO know how to eat. They know how to come AND eat! This dessert is my version of coming, going, and in-between. If you haven't realized by now, your authoress is a loaf freak, a layered fanatic, and an easy cook. I like to make dishes that are colorful and can be made ahead of time. This light concoction is guaranteed to have your Italian Stallion rearing up and naying for more! Who doesn't like ice cream? (Get rid of the pervert if he or she doesn't!).

Line a 9 x 5 inch loaf pan with wax paper. Remember: the bottom of the mold is going to be on top.

2 cups raspberry sherbert, softened
2 cups French vanilla ice cream, softened
2 cups lime sherbert, softened
1 (4 oz.) can crushed pineapple, drained thoroughly
3/4 cup flaked coconut

Garnish: lime slices and mint leaves

Mix 1/4 cup coconut into raspberry sherbert. Press on bottom of loaf pan. Freeze for one hour.

Combine 1/4 cup coconut, pineapple, and ice cream. Layer it next. Refreeze again. (Getting good, huh?) Layer last with 1/4 cup coconut and lime sherbert. Cover with plastic wrap. Refreeze.

When ready to serve, unmold and top with lime slices and mint leaves. Fresh fruits like cantaloupe, honey dew, and grapes are beautiful around this mold!

NOTE: I do not change this recipe. The flavors of the three iced layers are fantastic, and the flavor of the coconut and pineapple is sweet and rich. Make a couple and serve with a side of Pound-Me Cake....in fact, you can make a Pound-Me Cake sandwich by cutting two slices of Spermoni and placing it between cake, or vise versa.

POUND-ME CAKE
OR
BALLBUSTIN' BUNDT-PAN CAKE

Serves 8

If anyone tells you that cake isn't fattening, walk away from them! They are not people who can be trusted! They are liars! **This Cake IS fattening!** If you are trying to loose weight, eat lettuce, not cake. But, if you think life was meant to be half-lived, you may eat angel food cake or pound cake. I won't do angel food cake in this book (the thought of an angel makes me sick! We are not pure and angelic in this book, no matter how healthy we are trying to be). So, if you want pound cake...buy it. **IF YOU WANT POUND-ME CAKE, YOU GOT IT HERE!**

I can see no reason to make pound cake from scratch. I want my time for "utter" things.

1 pkg. pound cake mix or any cake mix flavor, made into a bundt shaped tube pan. Frost in any way, with any thing! I'm not doing frostings in THIS book. This cake is so moist, you do not need frosting!

Prepare cake mix as package directs. Include in your recipe any of the following combinations.

1 oz. light rum
1/2 cup golden raisins
1/4 cup chopped pecans

1 oz. bourbon
1/2 cup dark raisins
1/4 cup chopped pecans

1 oz. orange liqueur
1/2 cup low-sugar orange marmalade
1 tablespoon orange zest (orange peel), grated finely

1 oz. almond liqueur
1/2 cup chopped almonds

1 oz. chocolate cherry liqueur
1/2 cup chocolate chips
1/4 cup chopped pecans

1 oz. coffee liqueur
1/2 cup chocolate chips
1/4 cup chopped pecans

After cake is baked according to package directions, cool and frost. The cake is made just as the directions state, but add to the batter any liqueur and nuts, fruits, etc. that you like. This is the variety and what will make a basic just "okay" cake unusual. Frost if you want to. Lay back and get ready for your just rewards!

Note: Pound-Me Cakes also freeze well, so if you are planning to get pounded many times, make a few cakes. **Different strokes for different folks!**

WET DREAMS

Serves 8

This combination may not sound appealing, but when you bite into this frozen confection, you will experience no better rush in the world! It is sweet **AND** wet.

Crust:

1 1/2 cups graham cracker crumbs. Chocolate cookies can be used, but graham
   crackers are not as fattening.
1/4 cup sugar - no substitutes please
1/4 cup soft butter - no substitutes

Filling:

1 quart of your favorite ice cream or ice milk (Mrs. Boner likes coffee ice cream for this one).

THE MAGIC SECRET: Thawed Frozen Grape Juice Concentrate!

In a large bowl, mix graham cracker crumbs, sugar and butter. Blend thoroughly.
Spread crumb mixture on bottom and up the sides of a loaf pan or any other mold that has straight sides.

Soften ice cream and swirl grape juice into it. Press into mold. Freeze, covered with foil.
(Make it the day ahead.) Unmold, using a sharp knife, loosening around the edges.
Slice and top with **ANYTHING!**

Note: I really like coffee ice cream and grape juice.

SOME SUGGESTED TOPPINGS:

Shredded coconut
Chocolate sprinkles
Whipped topping
Crushed chocolate cookies
Chopped nuts

GOLDEN RAM

Serves 8

I do not know what a **Golden Ram** is. It might be a **BIG YELLOW CONDOM!** It might be a **GORGEOUS BIG BLOND HUNK** who does it to you! It might be a **HYBRID ANIMAL WITH HUMAN INSTINCTS!** But, let's just keep it simple. How about a pineapple and rum, ice cream dessert that is sure to satisfy **ANYTIME!**

8 pineapple slices. Drain thoroughly if canned. Fresh is nice, but not necessary.
2 quarts vanilla ice milk, ice cream, or my favorite: French vanilla bean ice cream.
1/4 cup light rum
Low-calorie chocolate syrup
Chopped pecans
Shredded coconut

Note: This is a great dessert to make the day before. All you have to do is assemble it before you are ready to serve!

Soften the ice cream and swirl the rum through it. Try to streak it through. Place back in freezer and don't look at it until the next day!

When ready to serve, drain the pineapple slices. Pat dry to get all the liquid out. Remove ice cream and scoop a large mound into the center of the pineapple. Drizzle with chocolate syrup, sprinkle with coconut and nuts.

SUBSTITUTIONS FOR PINEAPPLE:

Peaches, pears, apricots, or strawberries.

SUBSTITUTIONS FOR RUM:

Almond liqueur, orange liqueur, chocolate liqueurs

SUBSTITUTIONS FOR ICE CREAM:

NONE!

Note: Some fruits may have to be placed around the ice cream or served in dessert glasses because the scoop of ice cream won't stay on the fruit.

COULD YOU SHARE YOUR COMMENTS WITH MRS. BONER?

1. How did you learn about my book?

_____

_____

2. What is the occasion or reason for purchase?

_____

_____

3. Where do you think this book could be sold?

_____

_____

4. Additional Comments:

_____

_____

BONER APPETITE!™